Pocketful of Pinecones

Pocketful of Pinecones; Nature Study with the Gentle Art of Learning
A Story for Mother Culture
by Karen Andreola

ISBN 1-889209-03-1

Copyright ©2002 by Karen Andreola
Published by Charlotte Mason Research & Supply, Union, Maine

Illustrations by Robert E. Jones
Book design by Pneuma Books, complete publisher's services.
www.pneumadesign.com/books/info.htm
Editing by Nancy Drazga

Printed in the United States of America

Library of Congress Cataloging-in-Publication Data

Andreola, Karen.
  Pocketful of pinecones : nature study with the gentle art of learning
: a story for mother culture / by Karen Andreola.
      p. cm.
Includes bibliographical references and index.
  ISBN 1-889209-03-1 (pbk.)
  1. Nature study–Activity programs–United States. 2. Home
schooling–United States. 3. Mason, Charlotte M. (Charlotte Maria),
1842-1923. I. Mason, Charlotte M. (Charlotte Maria), 1842-1923. Home
education, a course of lectures to ladies. II. Title.
  LB1585.3 .A55 2001
  372.3′57′044-dc21

                                 2001008372

Karen Andreola's

Pocketful of Pinecones

Nature Study with the Gentle Art of Learning

A Story for Mother Culture™

Charlotte Mason
Research & Supply Company

Dedication

This book is dedicated to my fellow homeschool mother. She has taken the step, with her husband and children, to live the life she has imagined.

Table of Contents

Spring

Summer

Appendices

Introduction

"How do you do nature study with your children?" curious mothers ask me.

"We go on naturewalks," I answer. "The children draw what we find and sometimes we read about it when we get home. Their drawings and observations are kept in a Nature Notebook." Unable to go into more detail than this at a crowded homeschool conference, I point out that I have some chapters on how to do nature study in my book, *A Charlotte Mason Companion — Personal Reflections on the Gentle Art of Learning*.

The pages of *Pocketful of Pinecones* go further. They are meant to give the reader a larger look at a lifestyle of learning. Although the story is fiction, the experiences are based on my own. Since 1988 I have been doing nature study with my children in accordance with Charlotte

Mason's advice in *Home Education*. All of my children have created their own Nature Notebooks at one time or another and, I am happy to say, have retained a wonder and reverence for nature. *Pocketful of Pinecones* is written as the diary of a fictional homeschooling mother named Carol. Shall I admit that in many ways Carol is like myself? (Notice the similarity in the names.) Carol lives in New England during the Depression years of 1935-36. She starts her diary in September when homeschool lessons begin. The autumn section of the book is more didactic than later sections: the autumn section explains, step by step, how to construct a Nature Notebook and suggests ways to overcome certain obstacles that may arise. Gradually the chapters become less "teach-y" and by Christmas, as more of a story unfolds, you will be caught up in the drama of Carol and her family.

I like old books. Perhaps this is why I've given my book the voice and appearance of one. The message, however, has relevance for today's homeschooling mother. The illustrations were carefully researched and freely adapted from a style typical of the nineteen-thirties. Some pictures were based on specific works by George M. Sutton and George O. Richards. My thanks go to illustrator Robert. E. Jones for his faithful renderings.

⌣

You may have heard people in education talk about "hands-on" learning. What can be more hands-on than nature study? It is wonderful to have a bookish education if the books are living books, books written by authors who have a particular fondness for their subject — books other than dry textbooks. In a bookish education, nature study provides an opportunity for hands-on discovery learning. What is discovered is remembered. What is listened to, touched, smelled, watched, and (in some instances) tasted is better understood. Young children become keen observers. They develop the patient power of attention and observation when they use their five senses as amateur naturalists. Nature facts crammed from a textbook for a science test are more likely forgotten. *Pocketful of Pinecones* provides you with many examples of discovery learning — examples for each season. They are *merely* examples, however, meant to start you on your own adventure with nature.

Although the emphasis of the story is on nature study, it also touches upon a range of other subjects. It also gives the reader a brief introduction to the writings of Miss Charlotte Mason (1842-1923). At the back of the book you will find a supplement containing selected quotations from Miss Mason's book, *Home Education*. The quotations are referenced in the story because they are ones that were influential to Carol. (Carol had a copy of *Home Education*.) I suggest that you wait until the end of each chapter to read them — or even until the end of the story.

⁓

Last, but not least, *Pocketful of Pinecones* is essentially about the life of a mother who industriously cares for her family. Carol is on her feet a lot. She has worries, hopes, joys, and disappointments. She learns to trust the Lord in her circumstances. And she is very wise to participate in what I call Mother Culture. To take part in Mother Culture is to take a little time to keep growing. In as little as fifteen minutes a day, a mother can strengthen her spirit, expand her mind, exercise her creativity, or ponder ideas that will help her in her arduous task as homemaker/home teacher. I have designed this book to be useful for Mother Culture, to be nourishing, and to be influential in keeping up a mother's enthusiasm. It is my prayer that she who reads it will be encouraged in her task while she gathers practical ideas for teaching her own precious children by way of the gentle art of learning.

⁓

Karen Andreola
July 2001

Autumn

Carol Starts Something New

September 1935

Today I attempted something I've never done before. Homeschooling is an absolutely new experience for me. This morning Emily knocked on my bedroom door. Her golden hair was neatly brushed and she was wearing the new honey-colored dress I had made her. Then Donald shuffled in with a peculiar expression — his dark hair sticking out in all directions. He asked Emily where she was going so early this morning.

"Don't you know?" Emily asked, with purpose. "Today is the first day of school. Come on Don, get dressed."

"Okay," he answered reluctantly — probably partly because he didn't like being told what to do by his younger sister and partly because his attitude towards school has been one of utter dissatisfaction. With more wakefulness he added, "Hey, we don't have to go to school today, do we? You're teaching us this year, right Mom?"

Autumn

Carol Starts Something New

I hope I can live up to his expectations.

After breakfast, Emily was clearing the table and Don was licking the jam spoon when I came back into the kitchen with two black and white composition books. They're just ordinary composition books, but my plans are that the children will turn them into something special. Both children looked at me inquisitively. Don reached out for one of them — but not wishing to get them sticky with jam, I told him and Emily to come into the parlor as soon as their chores were finished.

I had their little desks set up in the parlor so that I can teach them in my favorite room. It's now a more cheerful room since the landlord allowed us to paint it robin's egg blue. The sheer ruffled curtains brighten up this corner of our rather dark bungalow. It will be a lovely place to teach the children.

Michael was in a hurry, as usual. As we joined him at the door to say goodbye, I straightened his tie and handed him his briefcase. However much in a hurry he was, on the doorstep he turned round to whisper an encouraging word in my ear, tipped his hat, and was off. I watched him go, thinking to myself, "What a kind man he is, and handsome too, in his new suit — matching so well his brown hair and brown eyes." Then it struck me that with his recent haircut and the cleft in his chin he bears a resemblance to Cary Grant. Of course, he is even more handsome than Cary Grant! I am so thankful that he has a good position at a time when so many men are out of work.

I was sitting at my writing desk squinting at a schedule sheet when the children came into the parlor. I was thinking to myself that I could have the makings of a truly orderly sort of person — though I know it will take constant effort. I have decided to use this first week to "warm up" to lessons — to acquaint the children with their subjects a little at a time. I think this will make for a good beginning. Emily is starting second grade and Don, fourth.

For science we will study God's creation together. I know how much Don and Emily like to be outdoors; therefore, I think the advice from *Home Education* by Miss Charlotte Mason — to have students record their observations of the out-of-doors in a Nature Notebook — will be enjoyable for them.

"Children, I'm looking forward to teaching you myself this year.

Carol Starts Something New

Come sit on the sofa with me and we'll talk about these books," I began. When I explained that they could keep a record of whatever bit of nature they found, drawing and writing a little something about what they observed, Emily was particularly keen on the idea. The set of colored pencils I gave her added to her anticipation. Don was silent.

When I wrote out a title page on a sheet of paper for them to copy into their Nature Notebooks, Emily sprang to her little desk. She began copying the words with her neatest handwriting. Don got up slowly, sighed, and after plopping his book on his desk, sank into his chair. At first I was mystified about this reaction; then it occurred to me that he must be embarrassed about his drawing ability. Then I remembered him telling me some months ago that some of the other students at school had relentlessly made fun of his drawing. No wonder he wasn't so keen on the idea of Nature Notebooks. I was proud of him, though, because he picked up his pencil and began writing his title page, anyway.

I glanced at Emily and saw that she was absorbed in her task in her slow, steady way, and gave her a "Good work!" To Don I gave an "It's coming along nicely," with a hand of encouragement on his shoulder. After these few words and the announcement that I'd be right back, I slipped away to the cellar to put some clothes in the automatic washer. When I returned five minutes later Emily was still at her desk, arranging her colored pencils in the order of the color wheel. Don was gone. I popped my head out of the kitchen door to see if I could spot him. Unsuccessful at this I walked into the backyard. I still couldn't see him anywhere! But when I called, he came out of hiding, relating to me that a group of children had been walking to school, and when they saw him he crawled under the back hedge. He decided to show me what he called his "secret hideout" — a small hollow sheltered by two forsythia bushes. Here I discovered the missing front door mat, which he must have been using to sit on. But before I could get out a "What's the idea, taking the door mat?" he called my attention to what he really wanted to show me.

It was the largest spider web we had ever seen. In the center was the fat hairy arachnid waiting for its prey. "Maybe a spider is something I *can* draw for my Nature Notebook," he said hopefully. I was thankful for the presence of the spider in Don's hideout, but I really didn't want the children outside during school hours. Nosey neighbors surround us. I told him that we ought to go back into the parlor and that he could draw the spider later in the afternoon.

When we got settled inside again, I introduced the children to their new arithmetic books. The first page of Don's book was quite easy for him — a good refresher for the memory. Emily, however, needed much help with her page. Therefore I took out our set of dominoes. This gave Emily practice at adding sets of numbers at a glance. I picked out the dominoes with lower number combinations. When she becomes proficient at these I'll introduce the higher combinations. While we were reviewing our arithmetic facts dark clouds blotted out the morning sunshine. Soon there was a soft shower of rain. The finger climbing motions of the old rhyme "Itsy-Bitsy Spider" were performed by Emily as she asked about Don's spider. Don frowned. I don't think she meant to tease him. It was just the association of rain and spider that gave her the idea of the song. Don resented such a reference yet admitted to me that it *could* be washed away. How was he to draw it then?

"Don't worry Don, your spider isn't in a water spout," Emily said plainly, trying to ease his mind.

Countenances were softened when we gathered on the sofa and I read aloud from the first chapter of *Bambi*. I chose this story because of its rich description of nature and plentiful array of new vocabulary.[A] They were riveted. I am happy I chose a story that they both seem to like so much, one that I have to admit I'm enjoying too.

⁓

By lunchtime I'd managed to put the washed laundry through the wringer and hang it up in the basement to dry — it was still wet outside. My brother had driven into town on Saturday and dropped off a half bushel of tomatoes, so after lunch I announced that I would be busy canning. Don pleaded, "May we go outside and check on the spider? It has stopped raining."

I nodded a yes, my mind on the work I had ahead of me. Then I remembered the clipboards I had purchased for their nature drawing. They were still in my shopping bag. Pulling them out, I showed the children how to clip on a sheet or two of paper from their drawing pads.

Carol Starts Something New

Next, a pencil was tied onto each clipboard and then they ran out the kitchen door, the clipboards clutched in their hands. In less than a minute they were back to report happily that the spider was still there and would I come see it again. Although I needed to get started with the canning I followed them. I knew it would be better to join in for the sake of allowing my lively children to share their sense of wonder.

How beautiful it was! Sunlight reflected off the tiny rain droplets that were strung along the web like beads. Even Emily, who normally shudders at spiders, thought it looked beautiful. I left them to their drawing (Emily remarking that she would only draw the web) and came inside to do my chore.

Just now Michael and the children are sitting comfortably in the parlor listening to their usual evening radio show while I write. It's been a good many years since I've kept a diary. I think I shall like keeping one again. And it will be a good place to record some of our new experiences with Nature Study. As the radio show draws to a close I will also close my diary with this: I think we had a fine first day of homeschool.

~

Don's garden spider — Zygiella atrica

~

Would you and your children welcome the idea of starting a Nature Notebook?

First Flowers

As soon as he is able to keep it himself, a nature-diary is a source of delight to a child. —Charlotte Mason

As I was filling Michael's lunch-pail this morning, I remarked to him what a beautiful morning it was — a good day for a naturewalk.

"Where did you come up with the idea to do Nature Notebooks?" he asked.

"You know that book I've been reading at night?"

"Oh, the one my sister gave you? The one she brought back from England?"

"Yes, *Home Education*, by a Miss Charlotte Mason," I said. I am so thankful for his sister's inquisitiveness. It was she who came upon the magazine *Parents' Review* and she who introduced me to Charlotte Mason's work. She was an amazing woman who worked with children for sixty years and developed a philosophy and a method of education that was used successfully with hundreds of children. "I've

been so inspired by what I've been reading," I continued. "I've only read a few articles here and there from the magazine so far, but her book has been so helpful. Without it I'd have so little solid guidance."

"My sister has always been one to dig up treasure," he admitted with one more crunch on his dark toast. Over the summer I had shared with him some of the helpful things I had been reading. I had told him about my plans for Nature Study, but perhaps I never told him about the Nature Notebooks. Or it's possible that I did, but he always seems to have something else on his mind — work most likely.

The children and I started off the day with spelling and reading. I asked Don to put a note in the milk-box for the milkman. I noted the words he needed help spelling and with these began a personal spelling list for him.

Perhaps Michael has been more attentive to my remarks about our Nature Study than I have given him credit for. There was a new book on Don's desk. Apparently Michael had left it there last night for us to discover in the morning. I knew at once that it must be an old favorite of his that he had found while browsing in a bookshop in town. When Don opened *Lives of the Hunted*, by Ernest Thompson Seton, and began thumbing through it, he took an obvious interest in the many little animal sketches in the margins.

"This doesn't look like a schoolbook to me," he said, after some inspection. I agreed, remembering the textbooks and readers he had

Autumn

brought home last year. I've been concerned about his chronic boredom for some time. His curiosity has been nearly "schooled out" of him. I am trusting in Miss Mason's remedy for this: her insistence that children be given what she calls "living books" — books that enliven the imagination and give children ideas to think about — books written by an author who shares a favorite subject or some first-hand experience with us.[B] I feel a little insecure about relying less on textbooks and more on living books; nevertheless my heart tells me to take courage and trust in Miss Mason's knowledge and years of experience.

We had few books in my house as I was growing up, but I remember that my brother Bob was given this very same book when he was young. When he finished it, I read it. Don listened with interest to my little introduction. I told him that Mr. Seton spent years observing and recording the behavior of individual birds and animals, and that he gave his animals names, and had a knack for telling about their shenanigans in the form of a story — a true story.[C]

~

Drawing the spider was a good warm-up the other day. It was a nice boost to Don's confidence to draw something that brought him wonder. Today their drawing was to be a more formal experience — part of my attempt at becoming an orderly person. I don't want to be the kind of person who is content with having good intentions, or who is too afraid to carry them out. Rather, I am determined to set aside the time to do what I have purposed to do and not be distracted. By afternoon the day was still beautifully bright and inviting. Before we went outside, I had the children place some drawing paper on the clipboards. I had decided that they should leave the Notebooks safely indoors. Next I explained that their drawings would be cut out and pasted into the Notebooks, and that I'd help them write their observations under the drawing on the lines of their books. In this way they would be making a sort of nature journal.

It was good to feel the sun on my face after being indoors all morning. I had Monday's wash to iron but had decided to delay the chore so I could join my children in some outdoor discovery. I also tried to take

my mind off the remaining tomatoes that needed to be canned and my
plans for supper. Perhaps I like being outdoors as much as the children.
I find it a refreshing diversion from the usual indoor domesticity. After
greeting Mr. Spider, we came to a corner of the backyard where a large
patch of tall grass was flourishing. Michael neglects this corner because
it isn't easy to reach with the mower.

   "Oh, look!" cried Emily. "Here are some flowers! Come on Don;

Autumn

let's draw these. Would these be good to draw, Mother? Don, you draw one, too."

I told her that these would be wonderful to draw, that the tall yellow flowers were called goldenrod and the blue ones chicory, and that I remembered how they used to grow all about the farm when I was a girl. (My father would take the chicory root, dry it, and make a coffee type of drink with it. But I didn't like his drinks.) Using a shovel I dug up one of the chicory plants to show the children the carrot-like taproot. I told the children that the chicory flower loves sunshine but will close its petals and go to sleep on cloudy days and remain closed all night. Like the chicory I soaked up the sunshine. I lingered in it, watching the children draw, then roused myself to go back indoors to do the ironing.

"Show me your pictures when you're finished," I said.

Not too long after, Emily found me in the cellar and approached me with a whine: "Mother, Don won't show me his drawing."

"He'll show it when he's ready," I replied. A mother's intuition told me that Don didn't like his drawing at all and was feeling bad about it. I didn't take up the matter. I was disappointed by the situation and needed some time to think about how to handle his trouble. I let him play the rest of the afternoon while I worked.

~

This evening I shared my predicament with Michael. He offered to investigate the problem. Don was sitting up in bed reading about Johnny Bear from *Lives of the Hunted*. I was tucking Emily into bed and reading to her from *A Child's Garden of Verses*, by R. L. Stevenson. What lovely poems!

Michael, meanwhile, went downstairs to the living room to seek out the contents of the wastepaper basket. He opened up crumbled balls of paper until he found the one he was looking for. He slipped it into his pocket, and went to see Don. He told me later what transpired.

Dad: "I'm glad to see you are enjoying the book I picked out for you. I read Mr. Seton's stories when I was a boy." Taking from his pocket the paper he'd found, he asked, "Is this yours?"

Don's head lowered when he saw it and he said, "Yup."

Dad: "Why was it in the trash?"

Don: "It stinks."

At this point, Michael told me, he suppressed a laugh.

"Emily is so much better at drawing than I am," Don muttered with discontent.

Dad: "Let me tell you something. You know that I was the oldest brother of four girls. Well, you know what? They all drew better than I could, so I quit drawing."

"All of them?" Don's sympathy was aroused.

Dad: "Yes, all of them. And if I had kept at it, I might draw really well today. I'd like you to keep on drawing. You'll be surprised how much progress you make, over time. Don't let happen to you what I let happen to me. You've seen my stick people." During the conversation he had been smoothing out the wrinkles of Don's crumpled picture.

Don smiled. "Okay, Dad." Michael handed it to him, and Don folded it up and stuck it between the pages of his book, promising to try another goldenrod flower tomorrow.

What a sympathetic husband I have! He handled the situation so much more calmly and patiently than I feel I could have at the end of this busy day. I want so much for the children to like their lessons. Perhaps I'm just suffering the nervous symptoms of a novice. Nonetheless, as I conclude this page of my diary I will pray to be less anxious about obstacles in our path.

❧

Chicory — Cichorium intybus
Tall goldenrod — Solidago canadensis

❧

Does your student like to draw? If not he can be encouraged to try and try again.

Giving the Goldenrod Another Try

T oday was the day Don and Emily were to paste their first drawings into their Nature Notebooks and I was a little nervous about it.

"I thought you drew a goldenrod yesterday," I remarked to Don.

"I did, but it didn't turn out, see?" He placed the crinkled picture in my hand with a bit of agitation. I told him that the goldenrod is a difficult flower to draw, that the drawing doesn't have to be perfect. We went into the backyard, cut some of yesterday's specimens, and brought them inside. I let the children know that we won't pick every wildflower we find because some are rare and need to be left alone. Goldenrod is quite common though, and because of this, it is often considered to be a weed. Emily put her chicory in a cup of water and was eagerly experimenting with her colored pencils to get the right shade of blue.

Chapter

3

Autumn

~12~

Giving the Goldenrod Another Try

Meanwhile, I urged Don to look more closely at his flower while I explained that it wasn't one flower at all, but many tiny flowers that grew together in a clump — a composite flower.

"Just draw what you see," I said, trying to encourage him, suggesting he add some of the stem and a leaf or two. Then I demonstrated how to draw the outline of a leaf. I had a lump in my throat as I sensed Don's lack of confidence, but I managed to tell him with a steady enough voice, "You drew what you saw when you drew your spider, didn't you? You've made a handsome spider drawing."

He met the challenge. It took him several attempts, using three more clean sheets of paper, and with me helping him to resist frustration, before he was happy with it. Then, with the satisfaction that comes to one who's worked hard for success, he used a yellow colored pencil and filled in his finished flower.

~

Emily cut around her picture of the chicory flower in a nice neat circle. I cautioned her not to use too much paste when I saw how much was on her brush. She was an inch from pasting her flower onto a left-hand page of her book when I stopped her with a hasty "Wait! I forgot to tell you something." Then, recognizing my flutter of nervousness, I took a slower breath to compose myself and told her that it would be best to place entries only on each right-hand page in her book, so that there would be pictures pasted only on one side of the pages. I explained that the pages would turn more easily this way. Phew!

~

Both children wrote the name of their flower at the left and the date on the right. I spelled the names of the flowers for them and then asked them what they had observed about them. The observations were to go underneath the drawing. Emily dictated to me a few words about her chicory. Then she copied them into her book from what I had written out for her.

When Don finished with his flower page he took the initiative to

cut and paste his spider into his book as well. He seemed pleased with his work. I acknowledged their accomplishment with a "Well done." What a relief it was to hear Don say, "This isn't going to be so bad after all!"

Perhaps I was a little nervous today because I'm not exactly sure of what I am doing or how it will all turn out. Nevertheless I have hopes that each day will bring me a little closer to my goal.

~

Giving the Goldenrod Another Try

This evening we all sat in the parlor. As Emily's favorite radio show, "Little Orphan Annie," was ending, I looked out at the sky. I think I look at the sky more than I do at the clock. The sunset left a pink horizon that managed enough of a glow to be noticed between the houses across the street. "Red sky at night is a sailor's delight," I wanted to say out loud but didn't as the radio show wasn't quite over. Instead I went back to knitting a mitten. I am finally getting around to using the red wool that Bob's wife, Dora, gave me.

Michael was in his armchair reading the newspaper. As it was just about the children's bedtime, he opened his Bible and read aloud a paragraph of Scripture. Then, giving me an unobtrusive wink, he asked to see the Nature Notebooks. He had privately received my good report.

"Oh these are capital pictures, just capital!" he told them, his arm around Don, who was leaning against his father. It was a rare treat to hear Michael use a word from his boyhood.

As I write, everyone is asleep. I have just finished re-reading the following passage from *Home Education*:

Mothers and Teachers Should Know About Nature: The mother cannot devote herself too much to this kind of reading, not only that she may read tid-bits to the children about matters they have come across, but that she may be able to answer their queries and direct their observations.... Any woman who is likely to spend an hour or two in the society of children, should make herself mistress of this sort of information; the children will adore her for knowing what they want to know, and who knows but she may give its bent for life to some young mind destined to do great things for the world.[1]

～

I think I will need to go downtown to Main Street to begin a search for field guides and a handbook for teachers of nature. Reflecting upon the week, perhaps Tuesdays will not do for neighborhood nature investigation, since it is ironing day. Wednesday afternoons may do better for our naturewalks. I will close for the night as I've stayed awake much too long.

Which afternoon of the week would be most suitable for your nature observation?

A Big Book on Order

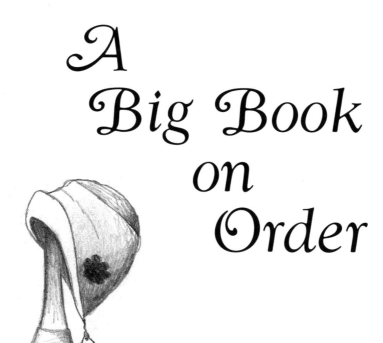

Today I had the whole of Saturday afternoon to myself. Michael had to go into work in the morning but was home with the children by lunchtime. My hair had just the right amount of curl in it for window-shopping and I had on one of my nicer dresses. I took the trolley to the far end of Main Street. It was a cool, bright, sunny day, a perfect day for window-shopping. It felt so freeing to have gotten all my chores at home completed and to be able to meander up and down Main Street for a couple hours of carefree leisure. After eyeing the new hats in Mrs. Swan's dress shop and the confectioneries next door, I made my way into the bookshop.

The clerk understood just what I was looking for, and handed me some field guides. He also recommended the *Handbook of Nature Study* by Anna Botsford Comstock. He told me that Miss Comstock had passed away in 1930

Chapter
4

— not long ago — but that her book has been an enormous source of information for teachers since its first printing in 1911. He hadn't any in the shop, he said, but he could special-order it for me. It is a large, expensive hardcover book of eight hundred pages or so. I felt my face flush when I agreed to have him order it for me. At the same time, however, I felt a thrill of anticipation. I love books, and I defended myself for the expense by reminding myself that this was a book I needed and probably would get much use out of.

After browsing the shelves awhile, an inexpensive little book full of illustrations on the life of Johnny Appleseed seemed to call out to me to buy it. So I did. I am certain the public library doesn't have a copy. I've scoured their shelves often enough to know.

Embarking for home, I stepped into Mrs. Swan's hat shop. There was the most darling winter hat in the window and I had to get a closer look at it. I think I've seen such a hat worn by Greta Garbo in the pictures. Even though I admired it I resisted even trying it on when I flipped over the price tag. The old adage, "Wear the old coat, buy the new book," came to mind. It seems particularly relevant to the efforts of those who are home educating. Next door, I picked out a small bag of sweets for my sweethearts and went on my way. It was a lovely afternoon.

When I returned my hair felt windswept and my feet felt sore from my long walk. But in greeting me at the door, Michael, in a funny creative way, gave me a compliment. "Welcome home, my pretty country girl," he said, putting his arm around me.

"What do you mean?" I asked, puzzled. He told me that it was good to see my cheeks pink and my countenance so refreshed.

~

Field guides are indispensable for identifying living things. What other books on nature do you have handy? The Handbook of Nature Study *is still in print.*

Floating Fluff

I'm still waiting for my book order. Two weeks have passed. Meanwhile, Don and Emily have made new entries in their Nature Notebooks. Each Wednesday, when the weather is fair, they are given an assignment to observe something of God's creation, to write about it, and draw it. But the children don't need to hear the word "assignment." They only need to know it is time to appreciate nature. We've now ventured out past the confines of our own little backyard and neighborhood. We take regular walks to the large park that is in the same direction as the public library. Once there, Don likes to run and stretch his legs and Emily always picks a certain swing from the tall swing set and swings until she's nearly out of breath. On one such excursion we spotted bluebirds eating berries. On another walk, before we even reached the park, a breeze carried some floating fluff across our path.

Autumn

Floating Fluff

Emily jumped and caught a fluff between her cupped hands. She held it out to me, saying, "Look, this is from a big dandelion!" I spotted a clump of weeds growing by the railroad tracks nearby and recognized among them one of my favorite childhood plants: the milkweed.

"Dandelion seeds are long and pointy," I told her. "These seeds are round disks. Yes, they're fluffy like dandelion seeds, but these come from a different plant. They're milkweed seeds," I said, as I led them off the sidewalk nearer to the tracks. We stood next to the fence that was safely separating us from the tracks. I told the children to split open a pod. "What do you feel inside?" I asked them.

"Oh, it's lovely, so soft and silky," spoke Emily, almost in a whisper.

Don split one open and, holding it high in front of him, waved it energetically back and forth until a cloud of milkweed seeds floated about his head. "Let's draw these!"

I laughed, telling him that I expected there would be many more milkweed plants growing in this neighborhood next year from all the seeds he was helping the wind to scatter. Then I asked them what the outside of the pod felt like.

"It's bumpy," said Don, running his fingers over it. I advised them that they could show its rough texture by drawing in the little bumps. They had their clipboards held steady with pencils poised when Don recognized a rumbling sound and we felt the vibrating earth under our feet.

"A train!" he shouted with excitement. Sure enough, within moments it came chugging along with loud squeaks and a clatter that cannot fail to impress a young boy. As we turned for home, I made a mental note of the other "weeds" growing by the fence. I plan to visit there again.

~

Dandelion — Taraxacum officinale
Milkweed — Asclepias syriaca

~

Does your neighborhood have any weedy wayside blossoms?

A Congregation of Swallows

Lessons were over for the day. Bob had dropped off a bushel of apples on his weekly trip to town, and I had made four apple pies. They were cooling near the kitchen window. Don was reading aloud from *The Story of Johnny Appleseed*. Emily listened while leaning over the kitchen table, her chin resting on folded arms, staring at the pies. I used to stare at my mother's pies — just as Emily now stares at mine — and contemplate the impressive mound of something delicious under the top crust. I had placed the best apples in the coolest part of the cellar and was busy canning the applesauce I had made with the less attractive apples when the telephone rang. My *Handbook of Nature Study* had arrived at the bookshop!

After delivering two of the pies to elderly neighbors, we all set out for the far side of town. I had the children's clipboards inside my shopping bag. Once on Main Street

Chapter
6

Autumn
~21~

we hopped on a trolley. This put a little fun into the children's day. At the bookshop I was handed my new book at the counter and stood there for a few moments thumbing through various sections of the book with approval. What a wonderful book! It looked to be brimming with ideas, but... on to the park. I could sit on a bench and examine it more closely while the children explored. When we left the bookshop and walked past Mrs. Swan's window I noticed that "my" hat was gone. Somehow, it didn't seem to make any difference to me.

As we came into the park by the north entrance, the children, running ahead, exchanged greetings with Patrick Murphy. Patrick, a boyhood friend of Michael's, is the gardener. The children like this corner of the park because it has an old barn where Patrick keeps the gardening tools, wheelbarrow, lawn mower, etc. The barn is the last bit of evidence that this city was once farmland. It reminds Don and Emily of their Uncle Bob's barn.

"It's pretty noisy here today in your park, Mr. Murphy," said Emily. He smiled. The children have a tradition of calling it *his* park and he thinks it funny. Don commented on the delirious birds overhead, remarking, "We don't usually hear this many birds singing." The children stretched their necks, lifting their chins in order to look almost straight above them, and watched the way the birds swooped and dove. The swallows had come together to migrate south to warmer weather.

Emily simply said, "They're lovely."

"Swallows are graceful, aren't they?" I put in, as I sat on the bench with my new book on my lap. Emily wanted to draw them but complained that they were moving around too much.

"Draw the ones sitting on the wire," I advised. While the children drew, I was able to look more closely at my book, which appears to be an assembly of more lessons than one teacher could ever be expected to teach. Each lesson presents pertinent information on the topic being studied — whether it be a particular plant, bird, insect, or star constellation. Thus, a teacher should be able to acquaint herself with any number of topics, as Charlotte Mason wrote to do. The lessons contain a list of questions to use to guide the students in observing various aspects of their "find." The lessons were originally written as a correspondence course, which accounts for the informal, chatty communication meant

A Congregation of Swallows

for those untrained in sciences. Perfect for me. On one page the author encourages the keeping of a field notebook: "These books, of whatever quality, are precious beyond price to their owners. And why not? For they represent what cannot be bought or sold, personal experience in the happy world of out-of-doors."[1] Here Miss Comstock and Miss Mason are in agreement, except that Miss Comstock thought that no child should be compelled to keep a field notebook, and Miss Mason required each student to keep a Nature Notebook in the normal course of things.

Finding the pages that told about swallows and swifts, I was able to put my new book to use at once. I asked the children to notice the swallow's tail as it was in flight. "Can you tell what the swallows are eating?" I asked. They were able to answer questions about things we hadn't ever noticed before.

"You're still watching these barn swallows, are you?" Patrick asked, returning with a pair of garden shears in one hand and a bag of clippings in another.

"Are they *barn* swallows because they live in your barn?" Don asked. Then it struck me. Don is questioning again! This is evidence that his curiosity has been sparked anew. Perhaps he had stopped asking questions while attending grammar school because school was doing all the asking of questions. Why should *he* ask anymore? I was secretly happy for him. Patrick explained that the barn swallows use a barn only in the spring and summer, when they build mud nests on the beams. The tree swallows had already left some weeks ago for their journey south. We followed him into the barn. We were looking for old nests. When we stepped inside the dimly lit barn we had to wait until our eyes refocused, but in just minutes Emily called out excitedly, "I see some!"

A little later, when the children had completed their swallow drawings, they showed them to Patrick. "These are capital!" he said, with a ring of honest admiration. The children's eyes met, astonished to hear that word again.

"That's just what Dad says about our pictures!" said Don.

"Your Dad and I have some things in common," he responded. I'm grateful for Patrick's willingness to answer questions and to care enough to share his knowledge and enthusiasm of nature with the children. I'm beginning to see that teaching and learning can take place outside the classroom. Therefore I am becoming a degree more comfortable about our homeschool experience.

～

Barn swallow — Hirundo rustica
Tree swallow — Iridoprocne bicolor

～

Is there a park in your town that you can visit?
You might find something new there.

Fancy That

October 1935

Our Nature Notebook project has led the children to become keen observers of nature. Although they draw similar things, their books reflect individual tastes. For example, when they collected and drew autumn leaves, Emily collected yellow-orange maple leaves and Don preferred the yellow birch leaves and the red-brown oak leaves. Both children liked making leaf rubbings. I decided these could be added to their Notebooks.

Here is how we did it. We placed a leaf face down on the table so that the back of the leaf — the side with the most relief — would be in contact with our paper, which is placed on top of the leaf. Then, with one hand we rubbed the side of a peeled crayon over the leaf, pressing firmly from the stem outward. With the other hand we held onto the stem through the paper to keep the leaf in place.

Chapter

7

Fancy That

Another day Emily drew little orange marigolds but Don chose to draw the bull thistle — the six-foot-tall flower with New England's largest thorns that we found growing along the fence next to the train tracks.

I've noticed that Don has an awareness of things that move and Emily likes things that are soft and lovely. Today Don found an interesting specimen that satisfied both his sister's fancy and his own. We were walking along the sidewalk to the corner drugstore to get a *Saturday Evening Post* — an occasional treat in which I indulge myself — when we suddenly stopped just before the store to look overhead at a canopy of golden leaves glowing and shimmering in the breeze. Two very large maple trees stand, like seasoned sentinels, one on each side of the door of a three-colored Victorian house. The trees add impressive beauty to the street. Butter-colored sunlight filtered through the canopy as we stooped to collect its shedding leaves of gold. "Isn't it wonderful that God would think of making something as beautiful as a tree for us to enjoy?" I asked Don and Emily. Again I pointed up at the arches of bright branches above us.[D]

"Yup," they answered almost in unison. Don noticed how the sidewalk squares bulged and slanted, heaved out of their places by the trees' powerful roots.

It was here along the slanting sidewalk that Don spotted the hairy caterpillar, affectionately called a woolly bear. It was boldly and conspicuously crossing our path. When Don scooped it up with a leaf, it curled up.

We all agreed to go home directly, in order to make the woolly bear an entry for the Nature Notebooks. (I forgot about getting my *Saturday Evening Post*.) When it was brought inside and left alone on the table, it uncurled and started traveling again. Emily exclaimed, with a giggle, that it was "cute and fuzzy." The caterpillar is reddish brown in the middle and black on both ends. I told them it was the larva stage of the Isabella tiger moth, and showed them a picture of the moth in my field guide. Miss Comstock's *Handbook* said the woolly-bear could be kept in a cool place — such as a cellar or a garage — to hibernate all winter. At the end of the afternoon, however, we set ours free.

Although lessons are always scheduled, I've learned to take advan-

Fancy That

tage of what nature brings to us outside of that schedule. This poem by
Christina Rossetti reflects our sentiments exactly:

> Brown and furry
> Caterpillar in a hurry
> Take your walk
> To the shady leaf, or stalk,
> Or what not,
> Which may be the chosen spot.
> No toad spy you,
> Hovering bird of prey pass by you;
> Spin and die,
> To live again a butterfly.

~

Woolly Bear — Isia isabella
Bull thistle — Cirsium vulgaris
Norway maple — Acer platanoides
Red maple — Acer rubrum
Northern red oak — Quercus rubra
White birch — Betula papyrifera

~

Have you tried making leaf rubbings? A leaf rubbing makes a lovely piece of stationary.

Keep your eyes open for a caterpillar crossing the street or sidewalk in autumn.

What Education Is All About

Reading one of the articles about education in one of the magazines my sister-in-law gave me has provided me with a new goal. Presently I aim to give the children three opportunities in our little homeschool every day as I am able: 1) something or someone to love, 2) something to do, and 3) something to think about. The article simply stated that this is what education is all about. Of course both children love their dad — and Uncle Bob and Aunt Dora — and Don faithfully takes care of his goldfish. I've tried to lead them to respect the elderly in their neighborhood and give gifts to those who are struggling with hard times. The reading of good books as well as their Nature Study provides them with something to think about. As far as something to do, last ironing day I showed them how to make window decorations by ironing colorful leaves between wax paper. Another day I showed them how to save the seeds from the marigold flowers that had finished blooming. The children folded paper to make their own seed packets, and before these homemade envelopes were filled with the little black marigold seeds, they were decorated on the front with a drawing of the flower. Certain elderly neighbors on the block were happy to receive these packets when we came to call. Dad, who has never acquired the confident skills of a handyman, nevertheless has a hammer, some nails, and a saw. With these, he and Don managed a rough construction of a bird feeder, which now hangs from the roof of the side porch.

~

Marigolds — Tagettes

~

Do your children have someone or something to love, something to do, and something to think about each day?

Contraptions

This afternoon, after filling my shopping bag with some needed groceries, we walked from the grocery store over to the park, just a few blocks away. Compared to our tiny back yard, the park provides a wealth of subjects. Often I let the children make their own discoveries, only occasionally pointing out things to them. Sometimes nature discovers them first. A spider climbed up Emily's sock today. "Oh, it's nasty!" she shrieked. "Take it off! Take it off!"

Don perked up at the word "nasty." "What's nasty?" he inquired, with a boy's interest.

Emily pointed. "Get a stick, Don, quickly!"

"Okay, okay!" he responded. Kneeling down, he placed a finger before the spider's path. "A daddy-long-legs!" he announced with pleasure, holding it up. "He won't bite you."

Contraptions

~

Upon hearing the commotion, Patrick walked over and wanted to know what was the matter. "Oh, it's just a spider," Emily said, pretending not to be bothered by it.

Don said he wished he could take it home and Patrick granted that wish by rigging a carrying case for it out of some materials found in the recesses of the barn. The daddy-longlegs was placed in a jar, a piece of cheesecloth was draped over the opening, and a piece of twine was wrapped around to hold it tight and then looped over for a handle.

"You're very handy, Mr. Murphy. Thank you," said Don, with a beaming face. I was glad Don remembered his manners, because he doesn't always. By the look on Patrick's face he seemed to be enjoying his moment of being elevated to almost hero status, but getting on with his work, he picked up three cages and headed out the barn door — the children at his heels. "What are the cages for?" asked Don, to his back.

"This," Patrick said with a twist, lifting an arm higher to display one, "is the latest, the safest, most efficient way to rid your lawn and garden of furry pests." He sounded like an advertisement — the kind Michael writes at work.

"Patrick Murphy, you sound like the radio," I said.

"That's where I heard about these live traps. And I'm going to go try them out right now and see if they're as good as they say."

The children asked if we could all watch from a distance. He nodded a yes so we followed him to a secluded part of the park behind a stone wall, a place encircled with oak trees. There they were, the pests, hidden from the view of most park goers: three chubby groundhogs gorging themselves on red clover. I mentioned that we needed to be very quiet or they would run away.

"Oh, they look like Teddy bears," Emily said in a hushed voice.

"Yup, hee-hee, little grizzlies," snickered Don.

"These groundhogs may be cute but they will all need to be moved to a more rural location," stated Patrick firmly, eyeing the hole and mound they had made on the park lawn. I asked if he would mind if the children drew them. He replied that it was okay, adding that he hoped to have them captured in the next week or so before they went into hiber-

nation. I handed Emily and Don their clipboards and they went to work while I was appointed to hold onto Mr. Daddy-longlegs (as well as the groceries). It is certainly no overstatement to say that a mother always has her arms full.

Afterwards I told Michael all about our day. He said he would like to invite Patrick and his family over for supper sometime. I wonder what I should cook.

This evening I made it a point to look over the chapter on ground-hogs in the *Handbook of Nature Study*. How interesting it was to find an entire page taken from Thoreau's journal at the end of the chapter. I was entertained as I read of his attempts to tame the creature: "I sat down by his side within a foot. I talked to him quasi forest lingo, baby-talk, at any rate in a conciliatory tone, and thought that I had some influence over him. He gritted his teeth less."[1] Thoreau's writings prove that Nature Study can be quite an amusing pastime for grown-ups (like myself), as well as an amusement for children.

～

Daddy-longlegs — Hadrobunus maculosus
Woodchuck or groundhog — Marmota monax

～

What is it about Nature Study that interests you, the teacher?

Pumpkins

This week I've been sitting up in bed at night reading a collection of Emily Dickinson's poems. My interest in poetry has increased since we started our Nature Study. When the children and I visit the library I'll occasionally take a book out for myself. The first few lines of one poem have stuck with me and I have found myself repeating the lines throughout the day:

The morns are meeker than they were —
The nuts are getting brown —
The berry's cheek is plumper —
The Rose is out of town.

~

Pumpkins

The days are growing noticeably shorter. And yes, the mornings are "meeker" as the sun seems downright shy about waking us up. The bushes and trees are brown and barren. Birds are getting harder to find. We had another Wednesday of rain. I had been wondering what the children would be able to add to their Nature Notebooks when the answer was delivered to our doorstep. This afternoon, while I was upstairs in my bedroom, I heard the noise of a rattling engine outside. I peered out of the window to confirm my guess. Though it was foggy I recognized Bob's truck below. It was filled with two crates of pumpkins and bushel baskets of gourds, yellow turnips, and butternut squash. Don heard it, too, and was in the driveway in a jiffy helping his uncle bring in the vegetables. I was pleased to see that Dora had come with him this time. She is now much rounder across the middle. "And here's the biggest pumpkin of all," announced Bob with a proud chuckle, his hands full of vegetables, as he used an elbow to hold open the door for his wife. Dora blushed as she entered the kitchen. They are expecting their first baby in just a couple of months.

Emily sat beside Dora, devoting all her attention to our ladies' conversation over tea and muffins. Dora ooed and ahhed over my modern kitchen with its white aluminum cabinets and its bright yellow walls, though she has never complained about her old-fashioned country kitchen. She wed into farm life and still holds romantic notions about country living. I, on the other hand, like living in our big town and have long had the desire to live closer to progress. Dora looked very happy. Emily kept staring at her. Perhaps it is the way Dora wears her hair: her long braids cross over her head like a mahogany crown. I need to remember to tell Emily that staring at people is not polite.

Bob took the winter squash down to the cellar. They couldn't stay because he had some business in town having to do with their truckload of vegetables and they needed to be back at the farm in time to milk the cows.

"Have a happy Thanksgiving Day!" Dora said cheerfully, as they climbed into the truck. I watched them pull out into the street. As I waved goodbye I prayed that their truck would keep running long enough to take them to their destinations and back home again to Dad's old farm.

Pumpkins

I started down the stairs to the cellar to inspect the latest generous delivery and met the children on their way up, each with arms wrapped around an orange pumpkin in a sort of hug. They said that they had gotten the idea to make one of Uncle Bob's pumpkins a picture in their Nature Notebooks. I thought it was a splendid idea.

While the children drew I caught their festive humor and cooked us up some squash. I was decorating a platter with squash and acorns just as Michael pulled into the driveway. The kitchen door opened and closed with only a quiet click and a deep voice stopped everyone in their tracks.

"Mmmm, Uncle Bob was here today, wasn't he?"

"Daddy's home!" howled the children happily. I was so relieved he hadn't had to work late again.

⌒

I am sitting with my diary in the parlor while the children listen to their radio program and Michael reads his newspaper. This time of day has proven to be a good time to write. A little while ago I reviewed the pages on pumpkins in Comstock's *Handbook*. The photograph in the book made me wish the children could be out in a pumpkin patch to see the pumpkins spread over the field with the vines swirling everywhere. I remember the large patch my father planted. Bob and I helped him with harvesting. I mentioned to Michael that next year in autumn we ought to drive out to Bob's so the children could pick some pumpkins for themselves. He glanced up from his newspaper and nodded in agreement. At the end of the chapter on pumpkins, is a portion of a lovely poem by John Greenleaf Whittier. Reading it calls forth memories of my own country childhood. I will read it to the children tomorrow.

> Ah! On Thanksgiving day, when from East and from West,
> From North and from South come the pilgrim and guest.
> When the gray-haired New-Englander sees round his board
> The old broken lines of affection restored,
> When the care-wearied man seeks his mother once more,
> And the worn matron smiles where the girl smiled before,

Pumpkins

What moistens the lip and brightens the eye?
What calls back the past, like the rich Pumpkin Pie?

Oh, fruit loved of boyhood? The old days recalling,
When wood-grapes were purpling and brown nuts were falling,
When we wild, ugly faces we carved in its skin,
Glaring out through the dark with a candle within!
When we laughed round the corn-heap, with hearts all in tune,
Our chair a broad pumpkin — our lantern the moon,
Telling tales of the fairy who travelled like steam,
In a pumpkin-shell coach, with two rats for her team![1]

~

Orange pumpkin — Cucurbita pepo

~

Still life subjects of fruits and vegetables in season can become a Nature Notebook entry. Which ones suggest themselves to you?

She's Asleep, Isn't She?

Michael telephoned to tell me he would be working late tonight. He didn't say *how* late. I'm sitting with my diary at the kitchen table watching for headlights in the driveway, keeping a covered plate of food warm over a pot of hot water. The New England boiled dinner I made becomes less appetizing by the minute. Although the children have been my constant companions, I am lonely for some adult fellowship. I'm lonely for Michael. I cannot get used to his having to be at the office for such long hours. I left the children sitting up in bed. Don is reading and Emily is looking at some picture books as they await a kiss goodnight, so I have some spare moments to write.

This afternoon I was taking some clothes off the line when Don stopped bouncing his ball in the driveway and walked past me to check on his spider. He gave me the news

It's Asleep, Isn't It?

as he passed by again. The big wheel of a web was missing and so was its inhabitant. I'm sure its been missing for some time but he has only remembered to check it recently. Disappointed, he flopped down on the stoop outside the kitchen door, staring at the ground. Emily came out with a small pail of birdseed that she had scooped out of a big bag. She asked Don to get her the stepladder. "Mother told me to fill the feeder," she said, her words backed with authority. It is obligatory in our family for the older brother to be helpful to his younger sister, so I was glad to see Don give her a hand. But then he went back to moping. With his gaze downcast he spotted something: a bumblebee lying motionless on a bed of dry leaves. He called Emily and me over to see it.

"Don't step on it!" Don blurted out, because Emily nearly did until Don pointed more directly at the spot.

"Oh, how sweet she looks. She's asleep, isn't she?" Emily asked. How innocent and naive children are!

"I don't think so," I said mildly. Don gently scooped it up in his hands.

"It's dead," Don divulged bluntly, "and it's as light as a feather." Candor is another virtue of childhood. He carried it inside. We all sat at the kitchen table looking at it more closely. I got Miss Comstock's *Handbook* and kept it open on my lap.

We took turns holding the bumblebee tenderly between two fingertips, turning it this way and that to observe its fuzzy body and its jointed legs and its mouth, which, I said, upon glancing down at my book, could be used for both biting and sucking. I chose some of the questions from the book, which I wouldn't myself have thought to ask: "Is the hair just as plush above as below? How many pairs of wings are there? Which pair of legs is the shortest? How many segments are there in the leg? Do you see the claws on the foot?" Then I told them that our bee might be a male because the book says, "But of all the numerous population of the bumblebee nest, only the queens survive the rigors of winter, and on them and their success depends the future of the bumblebee species."[1]

"Is that why my spider is gone? Because it's a male and the cold air killed it?" asked Don. I looked up information in the *Handbook* on the orb web spider, but couldn't find an answer to his question. I had to admit

It's Asleep, Isn't It?

I didn't know. Anyway, I told him that he is bound to find spiders and bumblebees in the springtime. That's when their babies are born.

They drew the bumblebee for their Nature Notebooks. As it was motionless, it was much easier to draw than a live one would have been. I checked on the tenderness of the small piece of corned beef that had been simmering for part of the afternoon, peeled some potatoes, and cut up some cabbage, carrots and beets for our New England boiled dinner, stopping in the middle of my task to glance over their shoulders. Something was wrong with their pictures. The colors and markings of the bees were right but... "How can you use your pencils to make the bee appear to be hairy?" I asked them. "Remember how fuzzy you made the woolly bear look?"

"Yup," answered Don.

"You can do the same with your bee."

"Oh, okay, sure," they both said and went on to add little short hairs at the borders of the markings with the newly sharpened points of their pencils. It amazes me how Don has taken to drawing after having had such an embarrassing struggle with it in the classroom. Is it the making of his own special book? Is it the drawing of what he sees and not just made-up pictures? Is it the quiet concentration he is able to have at home versus the stimulation of a crowded and competitive classroom? I'd like to think the home atmosphere has something to do with it. Charlotte Mason did claim that as much as one third of education is atmosphere when she said that education is "an atmosphere, a discipline, and a life of ideas."

Michael, I hope, will be home soon. Time to kiss the children good-night with a prayer and turn off their lights.

~

Bumblebee — Bombus pennsylvanicus

~

How can a pleasant home atmosphere, together with the discipline of good habits and a curriculum that includes ideas (to think about) help your school days run smoothly and happily?

Autumn

Reading
with
Burgess

November 1935

Each morning I listen to Emily read aloud. During the first two months of lessons her reading went at a snail's pace. I tried to be patient. I make it a point to keep my mind from drifting onto all the many things I need to get done in the day while she hobbles through her sentences. In this way I have learned to exercise a calmness (like Michael's) that makes Emily think I have all the time in the world to sit with her. Yet I don't allow a reading lesson to exceed fifteen minutes, so that Emily's bright attention will be preserved.[E] On alternate days we've been going over lists of word families that she practices "sounding out," and I have her read familiar nursery rhymes and poems.

Sometimes I write a rhyme or poem on paper and then cut out a separate slip for each word. Emily puts the slips of paper together and reconstructs the rhyme, as if she

Chapter
12

were doing a puzzle. The following day we review the sight words from the rhyme. Enlarging her sight-word vocabulary this way has helped her to read more by phrases instead of laboriously sounding out every word as if she has never seen it before. I find the advice about teaching reading in Charlotte Mason's *Home Education* to be most sensible.

Turning my back on the twaddly text of the typical "reader" has made me free to find just the thing for Emily, apparently. The animal tales by Thornton Burgess in his *Old Mother West Wind* and *Mother West Wind's Children* afford her the practice she needs to keep up a review of words previously introduced and provide her with enough new words to make the reading sufficiently challenging. Each delightful tale has a moral to it. And as each tale is *eventually* finished, there comes the happy feeling of accomplishment in Emily that bestows upon her the momentum to read another. *The Burgess Bird Book for Children* is also a source of delight to her. Mr. Burgess obviously had a love of nature.

~

What happens when we spend time reading books — be they fact or fiction — written by those who love nature?

Squirrels at the Park

Emily has had an increasing desire to spot birds during our walks. With observation questions jotted down on a scrap of paper and tucked into my purse, today we were headed to the park to feed the squirrels. The air was nippy, the sky overcast, but having heard it said, "If you don't like the weather in New England, wait five minutes," I had hopes of a bit of sun.

Before we reached the park, Emily saw a blue jay in some low bare branches. It squawked before it flew away, leaving behind a bright blue feather on the ground. Emily darted over, knelt down, and reached under the branches for the feather.

"Isn't it beautiful, Mother?" she asked. But as she stood up she caught her sweater in the branches and, as she tried to pull it free, a thorn scratched her wrist. This startled her. When she noticed the drops of red blood, tears

Chapter
13

Squirrels at the Park

flooded her eyes. "Mother," was all she could manage as she twisted to escape the grasp of the thorn bush, getting the buttons of her sweater caught as well. It seemed that whatever move she made, she got more and more tangled. Finally, with one last effort, she was free and heading in my direction, minus a button, a strand of unraveling wool trailing behind her. It's a wonder how much trouble a child can get into in just moments. I comforted Emily with the usual restorative — a bandage out of my purse and the sympathetic gesture of drying her tears. It took me months to knit that cardigan. I hid my frustration as best I could.

Don, who is extraordinarily good at retrieving small objects, was all the while looking for the missing button. Minutes later he proudly raised a closed fist, announcing that the button was found. "What a nasty bush!" Emily commented, watching me gather up the strand of wool and swiftly wrap it around two fingers and tuck it into a pocket of the sweater.

"Actually it's a beach rose — one of your favorite flowers," I told her, redirecting her attention. "Come spring this hedgerow will be covered with dark pink roses. Do you see these red balls? They're called rose hips. You can chew on one. Here, taste one. Aren't they sour?" I tried to show her that the hedgerow wasn't so nasty after all. But even so, better the bush be thought of as nasty than her mother. I think I managed quite well to hide my displeasure about the frayed cardigan.

The rose bush incident occurred one block from the park. Since the clouds had passed and the chill was chased away by amber rays of autumn sunlight, Emily didn't need the warm security of all her buttons fastened.

At the park, Don was first to spy the squirrels. With their paws, they dug into the grass with fluttering speed, pausing every few seconds to stiffly stand guard, then, assured that all was well, continued with their digging. One squirrel jealously chattered at another who had just received a morsel of food, pursuing it around and up the trunk of a tree. Stopping at the first branch it twitched its tail in agitation. This dashing about was right up Don's alley. Of course the children had seen squirrels at the park before, but today, because they were planning to draw them for their Nature Notebooks, they paid particular attention to them. One of the squirrels was missing some tail fur, and in the right light Don and Emily were able to see how the tail of a squirrel very much resembles a rat's underneath all that bushy fur. Using my scrap of notes, I asked

the observation questions, and then pointed out what prudent workers
the squirrels were, as they buried nuts for winter eating, and how marvelous it was that they could remember the spots miles apart and months
later.

The sun was already low in the sky when we started home. A

Squirrels at the Park

breeze was picking up, swirling crisp brown leaves around our feet. Emily was shivering. She and I walked briskly along the sidewalk, holding hands. Don was not on the sidewalk: he was marching upon and shuffling through the drifts of leaves that had collected against the curb, thoroughly enjoying the crunch he caused. Before long autumn will be giving way to winter.

As soon as we reached home I set the kettle boiling for tea and placed a shepherd's pie — which I had prepared earlier — in the oven to bake. My mother fixed this dish after the first frost and I recognized that I was following instinctively in her footsteps. I gave my thirsty children a glass of milk, after which they went off to their desks to put the finishing touches on their drawings. When the kettle whistled, so did I. How glad I am that our late afternoons are no longer overshadowed by homework. Last year I had to be stern about homework even though the children were quite spent by this time of day and had had enough busy work in the classroom. While my tea was steeping, I found a poem about squirrels in the nature *Handbook*. When the tea was ready, I poured myself a cup. I took it with my book into the parlor. Between what should have been sips but were thirsty swallows, I read the poem aloud to them. I wonder who is its author.

Just a tawny glimmer, a dash of red and gray,
Was it a flitting shadow, or a sunbeam gone astray!
It glances up a tree trunk, and a pair of bright eyes glow
Where a little spy in ambush is measuring his foe.
I hear a mocking chuckle, then wrathful, he grows bold
And stays his pressing business to scold and scold and scold.

Then I read to them about Furry. Furry was a baby squirrel that Miss Comstock had taken care of and the story in the *Handbook* is actually taken from her own journal. Tomorrow I will take dictation of what each child noticed about the squirrels and help them include more written observations into their Nature Notebooks.

When the kitchen timer went off, indicating that the shepherd's pie was done, it seemed also to be the signal for the children to ask, "Where's Dad?" I responded to their inquiry with a tone of sadness. How unimportant I feel compared to the company, which demands more and more of him. Must he really stay so late, so often? I try to talk about it with him but when I do he says very little. He has taken to loud sighing and is thoroughly drained and noticeably fed up by the end of each week. He is naturally reticent, but lately his efforts at masking his irritability about his work make him more so. He shouldn't bottle things up inside so much. Maybe he is just waiting for things to blow over. I must keep praying for him.

⌒

Beach rose — Rosa rugosa
Eastern gray squirrel — Sciurus carolinensis

⌒

Can your children describe the peculiarities and habits of the squirrel?

An Unexpected Butterfly

No shade, no shine, no butterflies,
no bees, no fruits, no flowers,
no leaves, no birds, No-vember.
– Thomas Hood

I think these lines by Thomas Hood make a clever poem for this time of the year, but the children and I cannot agree with him entirely, because it has been unusually mild — with no breeze — this last week of November. That being the case, we all decided today was a good time to visit the park. I brought my mending basket with me so I could try to figure out how to incorporate the unraveled wool back into Emily's sweater. I was in no hurry, however, to solve that problem, and sat for awhile on the park bench enjoying a break in the week's busy schedule. Patrick was snipping some branches and his curious companions were with him asking questions. He pointed out a bulge on the branch of a wild cherry tree. He told the children that inside were tiny eggs. Then he cut the egg case open to show Don and Emily all the little eggs. "There is a young caterpillar in each egg, and if I let them stay on the

Chapter
14

tree they will hatch in the spring. So many caterpillars could eat all the leaves of this tree," he explained. Don was standing near a puddle of water watching a butterfly that was basking in the gentle rays of the sun, slowly moving its wings. It flew to the puddle. How extraordinary! We watched it drinking water with its proboscis. I thought that they only drank from flowers. Patrick and Emily walked over to the puddle, too.

He told us, "When the butterfly is in hibernation she doesn't feel cold or thirsty, but she is thirsty now. She probably hasn't had a drink in six weeks." I hadn't known that some butterflies hibernate.

"What pretty wings!" said Emily. The butterfly had chocolatey brown wings with creamy yellow edges beyond a blue spotted border. Patrick told us it was a mourning cloak. Emily spoke to the butterfly, saying, "I'm going to get my clipboard. Please don't fly away."

Searching for more egg cases Patrick instead discovered a swallowtail chrysalis and called the children over to see it since we were on the subject of butterflies. He further explained that not all butterflies go into a deep sleep like the mourning cloak. Some survive the winter as eggs, some as caterpillars, and others hibernate in the pupa stage inside a chrysalis.

The instant he was finished explaining, Don blurted out, "Are you going to break it open to show us what's inside?"

Patrick replied that he wasn't because nature should mostly be left alone.

I read that nature is not secretive, but will reveal things only to those who look. It amazes me how this Nature Notebook project has given us new "eyes to see." It has a way of causing us to look for things that might otherwise go unnoticed. I don't feel compelled to add everything we find to their Notebooks, but somehow wishing them to be filled with "finds" has made us acutely sensitive to the natural world around us.

~

After supper tonight my heart was warmed as I watched Michael slowly turn the pages of Don's Nature Notebook, admiring the work. Then it was Emily's turn. She sat on his lap. He was genuinely impressed and gave out his compliments liberally, because he is the kind of parent that is easily impressed at the capabilities of his offspring. Although their pictures are somewhat crude I am certain they exceeded his expectations. I like them, too. Since it was a Friday night, he said, "I have a treat for you. Would you like to go downtown with Mother and me to the picture show to see Shirley Temple?"

"Oh, yes!" they cried together. Although I knew the second feature would be silly slap-stick (I don't really like Laurel and Hardy), I knew Michael would welcome the comic relief — a bit of laughs helps one to unwind. The picture with Miss Temple was a delight. And my thanks go to Laurel and Hardy because after the children were in bed, Michael confided in me about some of his stresses. Evidently there have been great differences of opinion about the proper management of the marketing department. These conflicts have been the cause of extra meetings and discussion into late hours. Also, his bosses have once again given him more responsibility for the same pay — which has finally made him realize that he is now doing the jobs of three people. He said that he is looking forward to the Christmas holiday.

~

Mourning cloak — Nymphalis antiopa
Black swallowtail — Papilio polyxenes

~

Is there a nature center you can visit or a nature buff you and your children can interview?

~

The butterfly on the cover of this book is a mourning cloak.

Winter

Spur-of-the-Moment Scribbling

December 1935

Today is the first Sunday in Advent. At this morning's church service we sang our first Christmas hymn of the season. "O Come, O Come, Emmanuel" set our minds and hearts upon Christ the Incarnate Deity. I love the Christmas hymns. They express such appreciation for the Savior. But when, later in the service, a different sort of hymn, was sung, I took special notice. The hymn, "I Sing the Mighty Power of God," by Isaac Watts, declares the attributes of God as displayed through his creation. Mr. Watts shared his awe of God when he wrote this song. The graceful lyrics about God's natural revelation kindled my spirit this morning, probably because we've been spending more time appreciating God's creation. I'd like the children to have the same attitude of reverence one day.

When the service ended and the congregation rose

Chapter
15

Spur-of-the-Moment Scribbling

to file out into the aisles to exchange pleasantries, I remained seated in the pew, bent over a hymnbook. Rummaging through my purse I found a pencil and the scrap of paper that had the squirrel questions on one side, and began scribbling. Of course my inquisitive children had to ask what I was doing. Michael, standing at the aisle seat, gave me side glances, listening for an explanation out of one ear as he nodded to or shook hands with those who passed by. "These verses would be very good ones to keep in our Nature Notebooks," I explained to them. My plan is to sing it at home and ask the children to copy one verse a day into their Notebooks.

I sing the mighty pow'r of God that made the mountains rise,
That spread the flowing seas abroad and built the lofty skies.
I sing the wisdom that ordained the sun to rule the day;
The moon shines full at His command, and all the stars obey.

I sing the goodness of the Lord that filled the earth with food;
He formed the creatures with His Word,
and then pronounced them good.
Lord, how Thy wonders are displayed where'er I turn my eye:
If I survey the ground I tread or gaze upon the sky!

There's not a plant or flow'r below but makes Thy glories known;
And clouds arise and tempests blow by order from Thy throne,
While all that borrows life from Thee is ever in Thy care,
And ev'ry-where that man can be, Thou, God, art present there.

⌣

Spur-of-the-Moment Scribbling

Natural Revelation is a doctrine of the Christian church. How has God made His glories known through the natural world where you live?

~

Keep your ears open for references to nature within the worship songs you sing.

Notebooks Put Aside

January 1936

I'm glad to have the opportunity to write in my diary again. I was extra busy at Christmastime and with my preoccupations, put off writing. We listened to Dickens' *A Christmas Carol* on the radio. I did lots of cooking, including baking dozens and dozens of butter cookies with the children, most of which we delivered to lonely neighbors. Day after day the kitchen was coated with white cake flour, as were the children. When they rolled the dough and cut out their shapes their round jolly faces looked like those of snowmen. Somehow they managed to dust themselves with as much flour as they dusted on the rolling pin and table.

A week before Christmas we invited over some friends from church and some neighbors for dessert and a game of charades. Michael got caught up in the game. He was quite clever at it. Consequently he looked silly and his children saw, for the first time, their tall figure of a father acting the clown. I was glad to hear him laugh. Christmas should be frolicsome, so the poets say.

Some evenings we sang together. Michael led us to look closer at the words to some of the Christmas hymns, such as Charles Wesley's "Hark the Herald Angels Sing." I had never noticed before how full of Biblical phrases this hymn is. Michael and I looked up the Scriptural references in its lines and shared them with the children. This made Advent season a spiritually enriching time for me. I enjoyed Michael's company very much.

Other than drawing a sprig of holly, rich with red berries, Nature Notebooks were set aside for most of December and the greater part of this month of January. Contemplation on "The Holly and the Ivy" has left me singing it now and again, even though the holidays are over. The first verse made a fine addition to the children's Notebooks. But I'm copying the whole of the carol here for myself.

~

The holly and the ivy,
When they are both full grown,
Of all the trees that are in the wood,
The holly bears the crown:

The rising of the sun,
And the running of the deer,
The playing of the merry organ,
Sweet singing in the choir.

The holly bears a blossom,
As white as the lily flower,
And Mary bore sweet Jesus Christ,
To be our sweet Savior.

The holly bears a berry,
As red as any blood,

Notebooks Put Aside

And Mary bore sweet Jesus Christ
To do poor sinners good:

The holly bears a prickle,
As sharp as any thorn,
And Mary bore sweet Jesus Christ
On Christmas Day in the morn:

The holly bears a bark,
As bitter as any fall,
And Mary bore sweet Jesus Christ
For to redeem us all.

The holly and the ivy,
When they are both full grown
Of all the trees that are in the wood
The holly bears the crown.

~

American holly — Ilex opaca

~

Take a winter naturewalk. Notice which plants
remain green and/or have thorns and berries.

Sun, Moon, and Stars in Their Courses Above

I am writing by candlelight in an upstairs bedroom of my childhood home. In the bedroom across the hall, Michael is tucking the children into bed. How quickly things happen. At noon today I received a call from my brother, telling me that Dora had had her baby, and that they had named him Jonathan. I congratulated him, and asked about Dora. He said that she had had a long delivery, and was feeling very weak. Then, barely able to get the words out, he said, "Carol, she is so weak and she won't eat anything."

"Don't worry. We'll come as soon as we can," I said. "We'll pack our bags and leave as soon as I can get Michael home from work. Make her lots of tea, and try to get her to drink it." Within moments of hanging up the telephone I began a flurry of departure preparations. I packed extra warm clothes for us because I remembered how drafty this old house is. The only heat comes from the two woodstoves on the first floor. A small suitcase was packed full of books, paper, and other supplies for lessons. Then there was the overnight bag to pack for Michael, a blanket to locate for the car trip, and a thermos of hot chocolate to make ready. "Yes Emily, you can bring Shirley Temple." It was the doll she was given at Christmas.

"What about my new tinker toys?" asked Don, half knowing what the answer would be.

"We can't bring too many things," I answered beginning to get flustered. I placed *Home Education* and my Bible on top of the clothes in my suitcase and considered the packing complete.

At last the car was packed and we were off. Michael drove more slowly than his usual sports-car-speed because there were shallow patches of snow on the road. The countryside is covered with snow. It looked so clean, white, and spacious. I thought the sky was never so blue against the white farmhouses, white fields, and white hills on the horizon. When we entered my old hometown of Appleton I thought how sleepy it looked. We passed the red schoolhouse, the church, and the general store, smoke lazily curling up from its chimney. When we turned down the rutted lane, the sugar maples and pasture fences made long shadows across our path and across the crystal snow bank on the opposite side of the lane. The bank sparkled in the soft orange light of the late afternoon sun.

Sun, Moon, and Stars in Their Courses Above

"Is anyone ever going to fix that dilapidated stone wall?" asked Michael, as we approached the house.

"Probably not. It's always been like that... maybe since the Revolutionary War," I answered, picking fun.

Bob had the front door open even before we got out of the car. He looked happy to see us and a little dazed. I gave him a hug and was met with the mingled smell of wood smoke, beef stew, oil lamp, and dog. Bob's hound, Reliable, in his excitement licked the children's faces and stepped on Michael's newly polished shoes. Michael pretended not to notice.

In the last two years Bob has talked about having electric installed but something always comes up to prevent it, such as a new roof for the barn, fencing materials, or other such things. Money can only go so far. But I am very glad of one thing — indoor plumbing. The bathtub now has two modern faucets — one with "C" and one with "H" on the handles. Only the "C" works. The "H" still comes from the pots and kettles on the wood stove in the kitchen.

~

Everything else is just as it always was before Mom and Dad passed away four years ago. The sameness of it all makes me miss them so. The oak coat rack with its mirror and place to put umbrellas is in its accustomed place in the front hall. The shadowy staircase disappears into the dimness. To the right of the staircase is the small but comfortable parlor. It still has the old piano, a faded tufted sofa, a grandfather clock, and a small Ben Franklin stove. Each of the two end tables holds an oil lamp with a globe shade painted with large roses. My mother's crocheted lace doilies cover all pieces of furniture. At the end of the front hall is the large kitchen, which has always been the heart of the house, accommodating much activity. There is the same, long, worn table used for preserving, preparing, and eating food, a wide pie safe, a china hutch with glass doors, an oak icebox, and of course the big black wood cookstove — iron pots and skillets hanging within arm's reach. The red calico curtains Dora made for the kitchen windows are the only thing different about the place.

While Dora was napping, the rest of us sat down at the long

kitchen table to eat. The stew was spooned into shallow bowls, and just as we were about to say grace, I looked up and noticed something white on top of Don's head.

"What's that?" I blurted out.

"It's a doily," giggled Emily.

"They seem to cover everything, why not me?" Don replied with a grin.

Sun, Moon, and Stars in Their Courses Above

"Take it off and stop being a clown," I told him. Everyone laughed, but I wonder what got into him. It must have something to do with Laurel and Hardy.

~

After the dishes were washed I found Dora awake. She was lying in bed in the cozy first floor bedroom off the parlor. When my eyes fell upon her white face, my mind made an eerie association. A scene from Dickens' *David Copperfield* came vividly to mind — the pathetic scene where Dora, lying abed, weak, ill, slowly dying, asks her husband's forgiveness for not being the strong capable wife she ought to have been. But *that* Dora is not Bob's Dora. This Dora will get better. I will see to it.

"Hello, Dora," I said softly.

Baby Jonathan was awake in the cradle beside the bed. "Oh, he's so precious. May I hold him?" Dora smiled, her eyes shining with a new mother's bliss. She nodded her yes. The children stood at the doorway peeking in. With a soft tone of invitation in her voice, Dora told the children to enter. I perched myself at the foot of the bed with Jonathan in my arms so the children could see his tiny face.

"He looks red," said Don.

"He's cross-eyed," said Emily. As if deeply insulted by these statements, the baby began to cry.

"Ah, this little cutie just needs to be changed, that's all," I said. Don nudged Emily.

"Let's go. Dad's calling us," he said and they followed their Dad's voice to the kitchen.

"Sorry Dora. My children need to learn more manners, " I confessed.
She was kind to tell me, "I find them refreshingly candid."

When I went into the kitchen to make Dora some tea and something more dainty than Bob's thick stew, I heard Michael and the children outside in the dark. I stepped outside into the cold night air and saw the faces of Emily, Don, and Michael lifted, gazing into the night sky. Michael exclaimed with raised arm, "The stars are so bright it seems as though they are just beyond my fingertips."

Sun, Moon, and Stars in Their Courses Above

"Wow, look at them all! Why are there so many more stars out here than in town?" asked Don.

"Do you see that sliver of a moon?" their dad asked. "When the moon is only a narrow crescent, the sky is darker and the stars seem brighter. You can see more stars when the moon is not so bright. Also, there are no street lights out here. In town there are so many lights that stay lit all night that they light up the night sky and then you and I can only see the brightest stars."

"What's the brightest star?" asked Emily.

"The North Star, sometimes called the Polestar is one of the brightest. There it is. Can you see it? The North Star is at the tip of the handle of the Little Dipper. The handle is pointing down. In January it looks like the North Star is the nail that it is hung upon.

"I can see it," said Emily excitedly.

"Me, too," added Don, just as excited.

"Now look a bit to the right of the North Star and you will find the Big Dipper. It looks like it is standing up on its handle. Some say one dipper is pouring into the other."

"I can see it," said Emily again, full of wonder.

"Me too," hooted Don.

Bob, who had just finished up in the barn, joined in the stargazing. "If you look long enough you may see a shooting star," he said.

Michael sang softly, still gazing at the sky: "The moon shines full at His command and all the stars obey." It was a line from the hymn we had learned to sing together. I love to hear him sing. And out in the quiet winter night (with no crickets to compete with) it sounded so clear and comforting to me. He seemed to be more at ease and contented tonight, observing the stars, than he's been for a long, long time.

"But Daddy the moon isn't full tonight," stated Emily.

Don interrupted her in his excitement; "There it goes! I saw one! I saw a shooting star!"

⁓

I was enjoying the moment so much I almost forgot about Dora's cinnamon toast. I served it crisp and smothered with apple butter, along with more chatter. Then I came upstairs to make sure the children were wearing both undershirts and flannel pajamas because just as I remembered, the upstairs was about fifty degrees. I piled the quilts over them. When Michael entered their bedroom, they asked him to tell them a story. I thought this was a good time to slip away in order to write a little something and here I am going on and on. I guess it's because I haven't written in so long. Not only is the ink running dry, my fingers are so cold I can't write another word.

~

Viewed from your car window, how does the landscape change from season to season?

~

Like Michael, many people believe the North Star to be one of the brightest stars. Actually it is only of second magnitude. It is considered the most important star. Can you tell why? Have you ever spotted the North Star at the tip of the constellation Little Dipper? The Big Dipper is not a constellation by itself. It is part of the large constellation Great Bear.

Uncle Bob's Barn

The adults rose before dawn. Michael had to get himself dressed and make sure that he set out early enough on his long drive to town to get to work on time. Bob had to replenish the wood stoves and milk a small barnful of cows by hand. I cooked up a pot of oatmeal and attended to Dora and the baby. Returning to the kitchen to crack some eggs into the iron skillet for Michael, I discovered he was already on his way out. "Gotta run," he said, giving me a kiss and tipping his hat. "I'll be back on the weekend. Miss you. Love you. Bye!" I could tell he was gearing up for a week of tense meetings.

~

Chapter

18

Soon after sunrise the kitchen was warm. The children came down and ate breakfast. I brought Dora some tea in a blue willow teacup, a soft-boiled egg in an eggcup, and the oatmeal in the prettiest china bowl I could find. I tried to make it the daintiest breakfast. Her little mound of hot oatmeal was surrounded by a moat of maple syrup. The napkin on the tray was one of a set usually reserved for holidays, embroidered in blue forget-me-knots by my mother. Bob, glad to hear his wife was eating, consumed his oatmeal in a manner that said, "Oatmeal is the best breakfast anyone could eat!"

Emily, sleeves rolled up to the elbows, balanced on a stepping stool to help wash the dishes. After the breakfast dishes were washed, it was my turn to roll up my sleeves. Armed with a scrub board and a tub of hot water, I washed diapers, sheets, and assorted clothes. I hung the clean wash on racks near the stove. My Maytag electric automatic washer with ringer attached is sorely missed. Emily watched as I put a ham bone, handfuls of chopped onions, four cloves of garlic, a bay leaf, and dried split peas into an iron pot of hot water. While the pea soup simmered on a back burner, I sat down and read aloud from *A Child's History of the World*. The author, who was a headmaster, thinks that children should be required to put the reading in their own words by narrating. This "telling back" of what is read is also something Charlotte Mason thought strongly about — something she considered to be the "art of knowing." I am following Miss Mason's advice in good faith because I agree that a child's wonderful ability to "tell" should not be allowed to lie fallow in his education.[F]

Emily is a little slower at forming the sentences of her narrations than Don is, but I know she will improve in time. Over the past weeks the children have been practicing their narration by telling back to me short fables by Aesop. I always read a new fable each morning, right after their arithmetic lesson — if there has been no dawdling over numbers. As they look forward to each day's fable, I have been able to subtly incorporate a certain amount of discipline into school lessons.

There is a chart in Comstock's *Handbook* that shows how certain constellations appear in the sky during certain months. Using the picture of the Dippers in the *Handbook* and their memories, the children drew their constellations and I helped with their writing. Don was especially keen about dictating to me details about last night's stargazing. I was happy that this gave him more writing than usual to copy into his

Uncle Bob's Barn

Nature Notebook. Lessons went smoothly this morning, even amongst all my washing and, after checking on Dora and the baby, it didn't seem long before we were out exploring the barn.

~

It was about fifteen degrees above zero this morning. All of the animals were in the barn. As we approached the old red barn with its weather vane perched precariously on top, the sweet smell of hay and not-so-sweet but not unpleasant smell of manure wafted our way. The barn door was partly open for air and light but as I pulled it aside fully, a ray of sunshine poured through the aisle, lighting up a haze of airborne particles of dust, hay, and feed.

Bob has a pair of oxen and one horse — a gelding. His name is Rubarb. At the sound of visitors, Rubarb stuck his head out of his stall and nickered a welcome. Dora's favorite Jersey cow, Belle, turned her big brown eyes on us, then demurely went back to chewing her cud. Her Angora goat, Cupie, put its hooves up on the door of its stall and bleated for attention and treats.

Uncle Bob's Barn

Don thought it would be fun to give the animals each a carrot. There is a root cellar by way of a door in the floor of the pantry. I told him that the vegetables in the root cellar were not to be used up so readily on the animals but that I would go and get one that could be broken into pieces. I only left them alone for a few moments. Upon returning I heard the nervous stamping of Rubarb's hoofs and I almost panicked. Then I saw what looked to be Emily throwing hay at the horse's face.

"Emily, don't throw hay!" I said rather loudly. She told me she was feeding him. I showed her the right way to do it and handed her a piece of carrot. "You must keep your hand held flat, like this," I said. I was relieved to see the horse had not been too badly frightened and was straining his head toward his favorite treat. I looked around for Don. Suddenly I heard his loud "whoop" and saw him playing with what I remembered to be a frayed piece of old rope hanging from the rafters. "Don, get down! Let's have Uncle Bob check it first." He came down reluctantly but obediently, covered in wisps of straw.

Handing them their clipboards, I told them to choose an animal to draw for their Notebooks. We were still working on their star entries, but I wanted to take advantage of the opportunity at hand. I sat beside them as they drew but then decided to have a closer look at the old rope. To my astonishment it was brand new. Their thoughtful uncle had replaced it.

In a short time the children's drawing fingers became stiff with the cold even though they had on their woolen gloves. I decided to break for lunch.

As we entered the kitchen, I saw Dora leaning over the table kneading bread dough and looking faint. She must have gotten bored in bed. I felt cross. "Dora," I said, anxiety racing through me, "I know you're not a Shrinking Violet when it comes to hard work, but you really shouldn't be doing this. You've only had the baby three days ago! Please go and lie down as the doctor ordered. Emily and I will do this." She gave me a startled, apologetic look and willingly went back to her room. I felt bad about the incident as I stood there watching her go. To have spoken in a calmer, more pleasant manner recommended itself to my conscience at once.

By late afternoon the temperature had warmed up to a nicer thirty degrees. The children spent a happy time swinging on the new rope in the barn until the sun began to set and it was time for supper.

Winter

~71~

Uncle Bob's Barn

Just a little while ago, as I tucked the children under their quilts, I was curious to know what story their father had told them the night before. They said that it was a story about how Southern black slaves would run away from a plantation by night, looking to the North Star to guide them. They would flee to the Northern states by following the Drinking Gourd — their name for the Big Dipper.

I decided to leave my curtains open tonight so I can lie awake and look at the Drinking Gourd. It appears that writing in this diary has made me greedy for candlelight. And as I see only a stub-of-a-candle is left flickering in the draft, I will close.

~

Have you ever thought of taking a field trip to a working farm?

Breakfast for the Birds

Last night, from under my own pile of quilts, I watched the stars twinkle and fell into a peaceful sleep. This morning there was ice on the window-panes. As I was finishing my devotions I heard a familiar pitter patter of little feet in the children's room. Don and Emily had risen early. But when, peeking into their room, I saw it was empty, I knew they must have dressed noiselessly and crept downstairs to the kitchen. I made haste to join them. Bob, stepping through the back door into the kitchen bearing an armload of wood, wished us a cheerful "Good *maunnin'*." He told the children to stay right where they were because he had something to show them. With a few big strides he was out of the room, returning in a moment with a lump of suet and a ball of string in his hands.

"What's that?" they both asked.

Chapter
19

Breakfast for the Birds

"This," he said while holding out the suet, "is the birds' breakfast." Don and Emily watched intently as Bob poured some sunflower seeds and cracked corn into a bowl. He invited them to roll two lumps of suet in this "breakfast" mixture, instructing them to press the mixture into the suet. Both children seemed to like getting their hands into the sticky stuff. When they had finished, each ball was a bumpy mass of seeds and corn. Bob wrapped string around each one, tying them up like a package.

After the children had washed their hands, Bob said, "Now let's hang them up." The children grabbed their coats, hats, and mittens, and followed him outside. I watched from the window while my pot of oatmeal simmered. I saw Bob hang the suet balls from a low branch of a tree near the house before he went off to do the milking. The children waited from a distance to see the birds come. They didn't have long to wait because Bob fed the birds regularly. I wanted to get a closer look at the chickadees. After moving the oatmeal to a warm spot on the stove I stepped outside quietly. Black-capped chickadees are one of the only signs of life in the bleak midwinter. When several of them flew over, Emily giggled. The spunky little birds jostled for a place on the ball. In a quiet voice, Emily mimicked their song: "Chick-a-dee-dee-dee." A larger black and white bird with a bright red spot on the back of its head swooped toward the happy chickadees and dispersed them with a flapping of wings. It was the hairy woodpecker. Don seemed to enjoy its intrusion. He watched it peck at the suet with vivacity. "The poor chickadees," Emily spoke out with sympathy.

"Ah, they've had enough," said Don. Then I stepped back into the house to ring the breakfast bell.

~

"Mother, we found lovely chickadees for our Nature Notebooks... and a big black and white bird... but they flew away," lamented Emily, as the two entered the kitchen. "How do we draw them if they've flown away?"

"We can find them in our field guide. After breakfast you can draw your birds using the field guide to help you with the markings."

During the morning's lessons the children listened to me read

Breakfast for the Birds

about the woodpecker. I'd like them to learn to recognize the drumming of its beak and have a chance to observe its unique hopping slide up a tree trunk. But I know that not all of what they will learn about God's creation will conveniently fit into my lessons. My students have a lifetime ahead of them in which to observe and discover — to become self-educated in their leisure, so to speak. My job is to allow their feet to walk the paths of wonder, to see that they form relations to various things, so that when the habit is formed, they will carry an appreciation for nature with them throughout their lives.

~

Black-capped chickadee — Parus atricapillus
Downy woodpecker — Picoides pubescens
Hairy woodpecker — Picoides villosus

~

A bird feeder filled consistently will become the "talk of the town" among birds. Of those that visit the feeder, how many different species can you identify?

A Gift from the Closet

Diapering is a new experience for Dora. She is slow and precise. With a ring of admiration in her voice, she exclaimed, "Carol, no matter how often or how swiftly you change the baby, you never stick him or yourself with the pins!" Only a mother would value such a compliment. I am glad that this particular dexterity has not left me. How good it feels to hold a baby in my arms! I wish I could have another baby of my own. Miscarriages are things one doesn't talk about, though it doesn't stop me from thinking what ages each of my "missed" children would be today had they survived.

Early this afternoon the rocking chair was brought from the bedroom into the parlor close to the Franklin stove so that Dora could sit up and visit with neighbors that dropped by with presents for the baby. Three young ladies brought sparkling jars from their pantries: strawberry-

A Gift from the Closet

rhubarb jam, apple butter, and butter pickles. I served them tea, butter-milk biscuits, and jam while they chatted and admired the baby. Noticing Don and Emily as they walked past us and up the hall stairs, one of the ladies asked how they were doing in school. I replied that I was teaching them at home and that I thought they were learning a lot this year, so far. I guess I gave her an answer she didn't expect because there was an awkward silence in the room until Dora tactfully changed the subject. Otherwise it was a delight to have some society in my day.

$\sim$

This evening Bob, holding aloft his copy of *Swiss Family Robinson*, offered to read to the children and tuck them into their beds. Since I was in the kitchen doing the ironing I had not gotten to that afternoon, I was comforted to hear their happy clamor of assent. When Bob came back downstairs, I had just finished the ironing and was clearing away my work in the kitchen. "I can't tell you how grateful we are that you came to help, Carol."

A smile broke through my fatigue. "Thank you," I said. "It's a pleasure to be able to help."

"Dora says she's learning a lot by listening to you teach the children... how you gracefully move from one subject to the next... how the children participate by telling in their own words what you've read to them. She says the books you are using sound very interesting."

"Thanks Bobbie, your encouraging words are as warm as summer sunshine. I wasn't exactly sure how I was going to educate them at home when the thought first occurred to me. All I knew was that it was something I wanted to try. Then Michael's sister gave me an old book and some magazines from England that have proved invaluable to me."

"But don't you have a big, modern school in the city that has an auditorium and a gymnasium?"

"Yes, we do. I don't know how to fully explain my desire to teach my children at home myself. The classes in the school are so large, and Emily was labeled "slow" in reading and arithmetic, but it's more than that. Don was losing his sense of wonder. He was bored. It seemed that his lights were going out for want of a better expression. Emily and Don

Winter

A Gift from the Closet

were losing a spark of curiosity and a love of knowledge that they had when they first started school. I wanted to get it back. And I think I am getting it back by homeschooling, and by following the principles of education laid down by Miss Charlotte Mason, the lady who wrote the book Michael's sister gave me. I'll let you look at it if you're interested."

That's all I said. I could have easily said more. But I stopped before I got too carried away. The words had flowed out of my mouth so fast and with such feeling that it surprised me. Bob must have realized how strongly I felt because he said,

"Sounds like God has put this on your heart, Carol. I wish you all of His blessings. Oh, by the way, when I saw Emily and Don's Nature Notebooks, something flashed in my mind."

"What's that?"

"Come upstairs. There is something I want to show you in the back hall closet."

We stepped lightly on the stairs and walked quietly down the hall. Opening the closet door, Bob tried to move the dusty boxes around without waking the children in the next room. I held the lantern. "Ah, here it is. Isn't this yours, Carol?" He handed me a scrapbook. Its pages were bound with twine, sandwiched by cardboard end pages, and when I opened it a flood of memories came to me. Page by yellowed page I examined the birds I had drawn as a young girl. I had collected them all into one chapter. Next was a group of pages dedicated to herbs and flowers. At the back were farm animals.

"How could I have forgotten about making this book?" I whispered to him in amazement.

He shook his head and said, "I haven't the faintest. Goodnight, Sis."

I guess some childhood experiences only return to the memory when one has children of her own, or in my case, a brother and new father to help in the reminding.

~

I polished the dust off the cover with the palm of my hand, but I was too tired and too cold to sit in the hall, so I came into my bedroom and put the scrapbook on the nightstand. The children will be delighted to see it. I will make it a treat for the end of the day. After quickly getting into my nightgown, here I write, shivering under the covers. I miss Michael. The middle of my back is aching. I should have prepared a hot water bottle to warm up this icy bed.

~

A dull education leads to a repressed initiative. In what ways do hands-on activities like Nature Study and the reading of good books help to retain that precious spark of curiosity that every child is born with?

~

Think back. Can you remember drawing anything from nature as a child?

Winter Storm

During the dark hours of the morning I was awakened by the roar of the wind through the trees. It was like the distant roar of a wild beast. The wind rattled the windows and howled a strange sort of musical scale. Emily was frightened and called for me. I hugged her and sat on her bed, quietly rubbing her back and saying very little, hoping not to awaken her further. She wasn't used to the creaks and groans of the old house. Don was sound asleep. Finally she turned over on her side, nestled her head on the pillow, and closed her eyes, listening, it seemed, to Don's slow, peaceful, rhythmic breathing. In a few minutes she had fallen back asleep. Very soon her breathing blended in rhythm with Don's. God has given me such precious children.

At daybreak snowflakes were flying and the wind still whipped around the farmyard. The wind seemed to be part of the morning's wake-up call, because I was up and dressed without even glancing at the clock on the nightstand. But the same wind that spurred on my dressing made it difficult for me to concentrate on Bible reading and prayer. During my quiet time with God in the early mornings I am more awake than at any other time. My devotions give the day its energy. I may skip writing in this diary but I try not to skip my time with Him who cares for me. It is proof that I remember Him, depend on his mercy, which is so thankfully new every morning. It is the evidence that I trust Him. It is because my days are so busy that I have kept myself from yielding to the God-can-wait syndrome. I need my heavenly Father and so I seek Him early. Prayers are the wings of the soul. They bear the Christian far from Earth, out of its cares, its woe, and its perplexities, into glorious serenity. It is the first God-ward step that the soul takes, so that

> *"Satan trembles when he sees,*
> *The weakest saint upon his knees."*

But this morning my excited children ran into my room without knocking, to point out how much snow had fallen. Devotions were cut short.

～

The wind was mischievously distracting during morning lessons. Instead of ignoring it I used its presence as an opportunity to talk about the earth's atmosphere. There is a small chart in my nature *Handbook* that was somewhat useful in explaining to the children how air currents swirl around the earth in what are called trade winds. When I also explained that the wind makes the temperature feel much colder and that therefore it probably wouldn't be a good day to be outdoors, Don's face fell. While the children did a bit of arithmetic, I mopped the kitchen floor. A bit later, Don, turning his eyes from his book to the window, commented that it had stopped snowing. By the time the morning lessons were over, the wind had stopped, too. All the land that we could see was completely still and buried in a foot of snow. But the sun was still hidden away and the dark grayness of the sky made the day gloomy.

At noon Bob could be heard entering the mudroom, stamping his feet on the slate floor to free his tall boots of snow. "Mmm, that soup smells mighty good!" he called out. Joining his wife, who was sitting at the kitchen table, he gave me a smile that seemed to say that he was relieved to see Dora looking less frail. I think my smile in reply conveyed the same thought to him. Don served the bowls of the hot, fragrant soup while I took some buns out of the oven, piling them on a tray.

After saying grace, Bob commented, "The snow is deep in places. I had to shovel it away from the doors. There were a lot of boards needing refastening on the poultry house due to the force of the wind."

"It's a wonder we didn't lose it altogether," Dora replied.

Wanting to serve the buns, Emily hopped over for the tray. The next minute the tray tilted, sending a cascade of little round buns to the floor. Her cheeks flushed.

"Never mind," Dora said consolingly.

"They're good enough for me," said Bob, reaching to the floor for one.

"And the floor's just been washed," I said brightly, taking a bun from the newly filled tray.

Meanwhile, Don, who no doubt preferred not to be indoors all afternoon, was bemoaning the fact that he didn't have tall boots "like Uncle Bob's." His chin cupped in one hand while he spooned soup into his mouth with the other, he was the very picture of despondency. I didn't comment; the winter gloom had bitten me, too.

～

After lunch Bob disappeared. For almost an hour Don had lolled against the kitchen table, watching Dora and Emily cut paper snowflakes, unwilling to join in. Our gloom, however, was about to be dispelled. Suddenly, his uncle reappeared at the mudroom door with a bundle under his arm. Don's eyes widened. Bob said, "Ever try playing hide'n seek in snow shoes? You can find each other by the tracks they make!"

"Snowshoes? Swell!" Don exclaimed, delirious with happiness.

"Those are ours from when we were children, aren't they?" I asked.

Winter Storm

"Hey, you remembered! I was beginning to think that you'd forgotten a good many things living in that city so long."

I gave him a suspicious glance. My brother knows I live amidst rows of houses close to a big downtown, but he always refers to Bridgeton as the city. He most likely considers the country a better place for mothers and children, but he is too polite to come straight out with his opinion.

Since Bob had Don and Emily well in hand, my next concern was to see that Dora took a nap when the baby did. Then I could start boiling the hens I had plucked. It seemed a good day for a chicken pie.

~

The chickens were simmering nicely in no time. My kitchen chores came to a pause after a pot of root vegetables were cooked and a large ball of dough had been made and wrapped in a damp tea towel and tucked away into the coolest part of the pantry.

"It's my turn now," I said softly to myself. I quickly put on my coat, buckled Dora's snowshoes onto my ankle boots, and escaped from the stuffy, steamy kitchen through the mudroom to the great white world outside. Reliable was happy to be out, too. The children watched him run off and started following, but couldn't keep up with him. But they found his tracks and trudged awkwardly after him, still getting the hang of the snowshoes. "I can hear him bark," said Emily. Soon they came upon some other tracks. "Look at these tracks," said Emily. "They're not Reliable's tracks." There was a trail of four marks close together with a space between them.

"Hmm, an animal couldn't make them by walking or running but it could hop and make them," Don reasoned, waiting for Emily to find the answer.

"A rabbit, of course!" said Emily.

"Yup, and Reliable is probably chasing it right now," Don said, lifting his eyebrows and smiling at the thought. They found the dog behind a heap of branches, digging in the snow.

"The rabbit has got to be under those branches," said Don.

"Oh," said Emily, worried.

"Reliable can't dig deep enough. The rabbit is safe," Don reassured her.

Reliable made a "woof" and ran in a different direction. They turned to follow his tracks again, and that's when they noticed me.

"Look, there's Mother on snow shoes!" The children had never seen me in snowshoes before, and thought it very funny. I laughed, too, watching their tottering, shuffling approach and the look of surprise on their faces. I was enjoying the beautiful, peaceful stillness. Because of the unbelievable quietness, the squeak of the snowshoes was amplified and the notes of a few twittering birds were distinct and clear. I was spreading hay on the ground when the children reached me.

"What are you doing, Mom?" asked Don.

"I am inviting some ground-eating birds to a winter picnic!" I replied. Then I explained that when hay is spread on top of the snow it looks more like the dark ground. I spread some seed around the hay and we left it for awhile, planning to come back later to see who would accept our invitation. We walked all around the farm together, around the

Winter

frozen, snow-covered pond, around evergreen trees — where Emily collected some little pinecones that were loosened by the night's wind and put them in her pocket. Then we walked to where they'd found the rabbit tracks. The children wanted to show me exactly where Reliable had dug. "Shh," I whispered, "don't move. The rabbit is under the pine tree over there." I moved only a finger to point.

"I don't see anything," said Emily.

"That's because the rabbit is white. Can you see it now?"

"Yes, yes I do, but why isn't it brown?" she asked. I explained to her about camouflage — why the rabbit's brown fur is replaced with pure white fur at the start of winter.

"Its predators will have a harder time spotting it, just as you did. In the spring, the brown fur will start to grow in and this will become its new color."

"A dog is a predator, right?" asked Don. Don started walking toward the rabbit but when the rabbit thought he was too close it thumped its big hind feet. It escaped from danger by running and hopping over the snow with amazing speed.

"Wow! Swell!" exclaimed Don.

"It's Thumper," cried Emily, recalling the story *Bambi*. There were some picnickers pecking happily at the hay-place. They were juncos. They twittered in a pleasant way as they ate. When the children came closer to the hay-place Don spotted some queer little tracks in the snow. Again he played detective.[G]

"Hmm, an animal with tiny paws ran here," he said, "and dragged his tail in the snow."

I was silent. Don gave me a quick, sly look — a look that meant he knew the answer to the mystery but was, again, giving Emily the joy of guessing. It was a small gesture of kindness but one that any mother would be proud to make note of in her diary because it was a mark of true gentlemanly thoughtfulness.

"A mouse," answered Emily, pleased with herself.

"Yes, it was probably foraging for birdseed, " I said and went indoors to put the chicken pie in the oven.

~

Winter Storm

When I peeked at the pie and saw that the gravy was bubbling under a successfully crispy crust, I opened the door to ring the dinner bell. But I never rang it because the children were already approaching, their cheeks rosy from playing in the cold air. When they entered the mudroom, Don asked, "What smells so good?" I didn't answer because I wanted it to be a surprise.

Unbuckling her snowshoes, Emily said, with sudden realization, "We never played hide 'n seek!"

"We can play it tomorrow," said Don brightly. I can't remember when such a gloomy winter's afternoon was spent so pleasantly.

~

Dark-eyed junco — Junco hyemalis
Snowshoe hare — Lepus americanus
White-footed mouse — Peromyscus leucopus

~

Some field guides reference a page of animal tracks. With such a guide you will be better able to recognize which animals have walked where you are walking, by recognizing their tracks in mud, sand, or snow.

The Walls of the Parlor Speak

This evening we were spending a short hour together in the parlor before retiring. Bob was holding baby Jonathan. The rest of us were enjoying the moment.

Dora had picked up her knitting, which always seems to be close by, and was busying herself with finely spun yellow wool. Reliable was stretched out over her feet. The layette sets Dora makes are sold to shops in the city. She doesn't get much money for them, but she believes wholeheartedly that "every little bit counts" — something my mother used to say. Dora has developed such a keen interest in knitting that she has rekindled great-grandmother's art of spinning and dying wool, using juices from the plants that grow within and without the fences of her garden. I thought of Emily's cardigan with its unraveled wool, and wished I had brought it with me. The walls of the parlor

Chapter
22

The Walls of the Parlor Speak

tonight seemed to ring with my mother's sayings; it was the wise words of a darner of socks that came to mind next: "Use it up, wear it out — make do, or do without." I'm confident Dora could patch Emily's sweater satisfactorily.

I was sitting on the sofa, my old Nature Notebook hidden behind a cushion. Knowing that the easiest way to get my children's fullest attention is to sit somewhere looking comfortable, I waited. Sure enough, in minutes they had made themselves cozy beside me.

"I have something special to show you," I said. "Close your eyes." They did so, as they've learned that the sooner they obey, the sooner the surprise.

"Okay, open!"

"What is it? It looks old," said Don.

"Let's take a look," I said, opening it to the first page, then turning a few of the others.

"It's someone's Nature Notebook," said Emily.

"It's mine; I made it when I was a little girl Don's age."

"That bird looks just like the one I drew. It's a junco, isn't it?" said Don.

"I like the flowers," said Emily. I told her that her grandma grew them all on this farm. The next moment I held my breath — Emily said that my cow had legs too short, like Don's. But Don wasn't perturbed. He just gave an honest chuckle. Over the months he had given drawing a "good go" and had gained sufficient confidence. He also found things to like about his pictures, though he knew they weren't perfect.

"How come you didn't show it to us before?" Don asked.

"I had completely forgotten about it. Your Uncle Bob found it here in the house."

"Then you'll have to show Dad," he said. That was Emily's cue to ask when Dad was coming back.

"I miss him," said Emily.

I think Don did, too, but he only said, "He's probably listening to the radio right now and reading the newspaper." I hoped he was, but I knew it was more likely that he was working late.

Uncle Bob carefully and inelegantly handed me baby Jonathan and sat down at the piano, saying, "We don't have radio, but how 'bout a song?" We all chorused agreement and Bob played a number of our favorites. I am appreciative whenever he plays for the children, because as a child I didn't take to piano lessons like he did.

"Okay, upstairs, children. Early to bed — early to rise!" I sang, echoing another of Mother's dictums.

"Would you read to us again tonight, Uncle Bob?" asked Don.

"Well, all right, but only if you both brush your teeth and change into your pajamas without moseying."

As soon as their footsteps were heard climbing the stairs, Bob told me that if I wanted, he could harness Rubarb to the sleigh and take me to the general store in the morning so that I could telephone Michael. I am so thankful. I miss Michael so much. I know I'll feel a lot better when I hear his voice. I hope it's a clear day tomorrow.

∼

Mind the Rooster

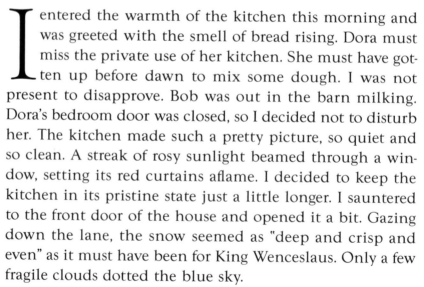

I entered the warmth of the kitchen this morning and was greeted with the smell of bread rising. Dora must miss the private use of her kitchen. She must have gotten up before dawn to mix some dough. I was not present to disapprove. Bob was out in the barn milking. Dora's bedroom door was closed, so I decided not to disturb her. The kitchen made such a pretty picture, so quiet and so clean. A streak of rosy sunlight beamed through a window, setting its red curtains aflame. I decided to keep the kitchen in its pristine state just a little longer. I sauntered to the front door of the house and opened it a bit. Gazing down the lane, the snow seemed as "deep and crisp and even" as it must have been for King Wenceslaus. Only a few fragile clouds dotted the blue sky.

"What a white January," I spoke out loud to the cold air, forming my own clouds in front of me. At that moment

Mind the Rooster

Emily and Don came down the stairs. "Brrr. Is Dad here?" Emily asked, shivering as she joined me at the open front door.

"Good morning, children. No, Dad isn't here, but after breakfast Uncle Bob is going to take me on the sleigh to the general store to call him on the telephone. Would you like to come?" I asked. Yes, they would, they chorused. They were very excited about it.

~

With breakfast preparations finally in motion, I asked Emily to collect some eggs. "Don, would you come with me... please...? That rooster is nasty."

"Oh, you mean Tailgate? He won't hurt you."

"Yes he will."

"He won't chase you into the snow because he doesn't like it." But Emily held her gaze on Don imploringly.

"All right, I'm coming," he said. I think it was the thought of putting on snowshoes again that motivated him. I must put in a word about Bob's rooster, Tailgate. At the end of his long decorative neck is a tiny head with only two ideas in it — his flock and his food. In his legs is the immense energy of a wild wind-up toy. But today Emily could collect what few eggs there were in safety, without feeling that she was spying behind enemy lines, because of the snow and because of Don's ability to distract him. Emily told me that she found the clucking and fussing of the hens to be a pleasant, funny sort of sound. And that she thought a hen would make a good entry into her Nature Notebook. She liked the one in my book. But Don said he'd rather draw Tailgate because of his bolder markings.

There were only four eggs in Emily's basket, but they were enough to make a short stack of pancakes for everyone. I noticed that the pantry was down to its last jar of maple syrup and when I saw how liberally the children poured it onto their pancakes, I asked them to be more sparing. But Dora said, with a gleam in her eyes, "Never mind. Maple sugar season will soon be upon us." As the last bite of pancake disappeared, she said to me, "Now, you just go on your ride to town. I'll wash up."

"Are you sure?" I asked.

Mind the Rooster

"Of course I'm sure. I've got to start doing something around here."
I yielded, and before we could say "Jack Robinson" we were riding in a
one-horse open sleigh down the lane — the cold breeze stinging our faces
— singing what else but last month's tune, "Jingle Bells," and as the song
suggested, we were "laughing all the way." Rubarb's mane danced as he
trotted. Country sunshine danced upon the snow. We squinted our eyes.
"Living in the country does have its occasional thrills," was just what I
was thinking when I met Bob's earnest smile with a happy but (another)
suspicious one of my own.

In the store, a wave of homesickness brought my spirits low. It was
good to hear Michael's voice but I could tell he was trying very hard to
sound cheerful. The telephone was attached to the wall and the children
were standing tip-toe on an upturned wooden crate in order to talk into
it while I was trying to put together the pieces of what Michael had just
told me. He had said something about large signs — called billboards —
along roadsides, that he disagreed with. He was accused of not wanting
the company's success — not wanting to expand the marketing department in innovative directions. Can I help being disheartened? It is so
unlike him to say anything about his job. And to hear something nega-
tive when we're apart sets me awry. Bob bought everything on Dora's list
and we started back to the farm. I didn't want to sing this time so I told
the children my lips were frozen. How can such a hopeful day turn out
so tragically just from a few confusing statements made during one telephone call? I must try not to worry. I will pray again tonight.

∾

*Different breeds of roosters and hens can be seen on
display at a county fair. Do you know what breed
of chicken laid the eggs you ate for breakfast this
morning?*

Sunday Icebox Cake

W e rode to church in the sleigh, scarves wrapped round and round our necks and chins. The children had hidden away carrots in each coat pocket. Upon arriving at the church, we left Rubarb under the long covered shed, contently eating his carrots.

Sunday is the one day of the week when a country woman can get off her feet in the middle of the morning. I set my mind to take advantage of this opportunity and to take joy in trusting God. I prayed to be relieved of my worry over Michael's job troubles. Through an east window the sun streamed in on me so that I scarcely felt the cold. I feasted my eyes upon the colors of the church's one stained glass window, which was positioned behind the pulpit. It was a pleasing winter substitute for, and reminder of, the colorful flowers of spring. In front of this window

Chapter 24

Sunday Icebox Cake

stood Pastor Bingham, a tall, dignified, learned man with glossy black hair and the same weather-beaten complexion, the same rough hands, as his rural congregation. His sermons prove he knows his Bible well. Instead of reading a verse he recites it from memory. Mom and Dad took us to this church no matter what pastors came and went. Before Daddy passed away I remember him saying that Pastor Bingham had the four graces: love for God, charity for men, purity, and humility. I had to agree, because this morning's sermon, so heartily and genuinely spoken, kept my mind on things divine and delivered me from mortal weariness.

Still, I wasn't really up to big smiles and light chatter. Courtesy, however, demanded that I mingle with the dispersing congregation. Just as I stood up my eyes met those of Mrs. Emma Cook, a widow of some years, and a longtime friend of my mother's. She was sitting across the aisle. When I was a child, Mrs. Cook was my Sunday school teacher. With a white, gloved hand, she patted the empty spot on the bench, an invitation for me to sit and visit with her. She was wearing the same radiant smile she had worn when she was my Sunday school teacher, only now it uplifted a very wrinkled face. Her attire was, as it had always been, a soft flowing dress with a lace collar, enhanced by a simple string of pearls — she looked like she had stepped straight out of the Edwardian era. Her white hair was the same also: crimped and in a low bun. There was no sign of complaint in her face or in her voice, though she had outlived three husbands — husbands who had succumbed to death from influenza, from war, and by tragic accident. Dora told me later that her three girls had moved out west and that she was left with no grandchildren close enough on which to fully exercise her affectionate nature. Mrs. Cook asked me about my family, how I liked living so near the city, told me that she kept flowers at my parents' graves, and that she was praying for me. In fact, she said, she had not ceased praying for me since she had first had me in Sunday school class. This unexpected reverse of "light chatter" dazzled me. I sensed a heavenly message of the love of God delivered through what seemed to be an angel.

~

On the ride home we noticed that the snow was beginning to get slushy. Bob said he thought the roads would be clear enough near

Sunday Icebox Cake

the end of the week for him to take us home in the truck if it didn't snow again.

"But Bob, should I be leaving Dora so soon?" I asked, while he unhitched Rubarb.

"You need to get home to Michael. We'll be okay," he replied.

Dora, who had stayed home to rest and prepare a light midday meal, appeared to be getting stronger. This afternoon she and Emily made a Sunday icebox cake, or rather, Dora, busy with the baby in her arms, gave directions, and Emily, delighted to have the responsibility of "cake-making" all to herself, was all too ready to follow every command. There is no actual cooking required for this cake — only assembling of ingredients — and Emily was busy finding and collecting everything she needed. I write the recipe here so I can refer to it at home:

First Emily placed a Graham cracker on a plate. Then she spread some applesauce over it and sprinkled on cinnamon. Four more layers of Graham crackers were spread with applesauce and cinnamon. Then the sixth cracker was placed on top. It took tenacity to whip the cream with the rickety eggbeater. To this she added a little sugar and beat it some more. The whipped cream was spread all around the cake. Chopped nuts were sprinkled on top and it was to be kept in the icebox for three hours for the crackers to soften into a cake consistency. Without Dora lifting a finger, Emily also cleaned up, washed up, then dried and put away the bowl and spoons. She had only Dora's attentive pleasant conversation to accompany these tasks. Emily was proud of her little layer cake when it was sliced and served on blue and white dishes, and her uncle told her it was "mighty fine." I was proud too. As I was eating the cake, I noticed Emily's pinecones on the top of the icebox. That morning she had evidently replaced her pocketful of pinecones with Rubarb's carrots. The pinecones have given me an idea for our next Nature Notebook subject.

~

Children have been known to fill their pockets with acorns, pinecones, feathers, shells, rocks, or even the empty exoskeletons of insects. What can be learned by studying these objects?

Tree Climbing

February 1936

lmost every morning I do washing during lessons. While I heated the wash water on the stove *this* morning, I read aloud some history. Don knew what was coming. The dirty diapers took priority and their presence caused him to ask, "Must we do lessons in the kitchen today, Mother?"

"Shhh, Aunt Dora will hear you. Yes, we must." My attention was divided between scrubbing on the wash board and Don, who was narrating a chapter of history, two fingers clipped over his nose. The same feat so necessary to mothers, of being able to do two or three things at once, was continued through much of the morning. I say "feat" because it is a learned skill, something that hasn't come naturally to me. I gave one ear to Emily's narration and the other to listening for any sounds from the baby in the next room, at the same time hanging diapers on racks to dry. My

Chapter

25

Tree Climbing

routine chores are not tedious because I find the children's lessons interesting and because all my work is done for those I love. But there was a moment in which I wished I were the one with the baby and someone else were doing the washing.

An hour before lunch I announced that we were going on a nature-walk. We were going to the woods at the edge of the pasture. I told Don to take his pocket-knife and Emily her pinecones. I carried the book, *Our Native Trees.*

The woodland would have seemed bare this time of year if it weren't for the evergreens. "Now Emily," I asked, "can you match up your pinecones with the tree they came from?"

After looking around for awhile, she said, "It's this one, the one with the littlest pinecones."

"This is a hemlock," I said.

"I like the ones with the bigger pinecones — those," said Don pointing.

"Those trees are white pines. Do you see how the branches grow horizontally? It makes a great climbing tree. I used to climb trees like this one when I was young."

"May I climb it, Mother?" asked Don, excitement in his voice.

"Yes, but only after we do some more detective work." I explained that the pinecones drop their seeds in the fall. Then I asked Don to cut a piece of branch with his pocket-knife.

"It smells like Christmas," noted Emily. Don also breathed in the fresh fragrance and, keeping the branch under his nose a bit longer, said, "I've got a mustache like Uncle Bob's."

"You look more like Groucho Marx," I joked. "These pine needles are really the tree's very narrow leaves," I continued.

Our little group of naturalists also identified some other conifers, cutting samples of each to take back to the house for drawings. Emily collected lots more little cones at the foot of a hemlock. I asked them how the branches of the hemlock were arranged to shed the snow. When both Emily and Don answered to my satisfaction they were set free to remove their snowshoes and climb a pine tree high enough to enjoy a bird's eye view of the farm. I stood below, wondering whether my own mother ever was as nervous about her children climbing trees as I was about mine.

Tree Climbing

Then again, most of my tree climbing was done when nobody was around to watch.

~

Eastern hemlock — Tsuga canadensis
Eastern white pine — Pinus strobus
White spruce — Picea glauca

~

Are there any conifers in your neighborhood?

Dora Puts the Kettle On

This week, although Dora has gotten her needed rest, she has been up more and seems to be enjoying getting back into her kitchen. Often when the children worked on their nature drawings, Dora was at the kitchen table with them. Once, with a brush and some watercolor paints, she drew some pine and fir branches. One stroke of a fine brush with green paint was all that was needed for each pine needle. She pointed out that the white pine always has five needles growing together in one cluster. One pays closer attention to things when they are to be painted. She let Don and Emily each have a turn at using her brush and paints, stating that she would very much like to create her own Nature Diary come spring. She told the children that they had been her inspiration.

Bob was looking over their shoulders and con-

Chapter
26

tributed his own bit of information for the studious group. Holding aloft a book from his boyhood, he read aloud, "All silver shillings and smaller coins that were made in the colony of Massachusetts in the latter part of the 17th century bore the picture of a white pine... In the dense woods the trees grow straight as an arrow. They were used as masts in his Majesty's navy...."

Bob and Dora would make more than adequate homeschooling parents. They seem to be quite taken with Charlotte Mason's gentle art of learning.

~

It is nearly the end of our second week here. I don't know when I've expended more energy. Much of the time I plod along lackadaisically, trying not to think how tired life makes me. I've been pretty successful until today. "Let me make *you* some tea, Carol," Dora said this afternoon when I entered her bedroom, hoping for a chance to hold baby Jonathan. Don and Emily were swinging in the barn. The cushioned rocking chair cradled me in comfort as I cradled the warm soft baby in my arms. I can't remember enjoying a sit-down more than I was enjoying it that instant.

"This is for you," Dora said, handing me a present wrapped in a piece of leftover shelf paper she had decorated herself. With one arm I held the baby and with the other I opened the present. It was a knit hat, quite pretty and fashionable. "Try it on," said Dora, reaching for the baby. The hat fit down around my face just as it was supposed to. When I caught a glimpse of myself in Dora's vanity mirror, I was a little chagrined to note that the lovely hat was atop a rather bedraggled mop of hair. My dress also showed the effects of my day's labor. I hadn't been thinking too much about my appearance until that moment.

Dora was full of sweet words of appreciation for all of my help. She told me that I was the "very soul of kindness" and added more words of admiration for the way I am bringing up Donald and Emily. I absorbed Dora's compliments like dry earth absorbs long-awaited raindrops. A sort of happy weariness came over me and I felt a whirlpool of emotions struggling within me, so much so that I was unable to keep my eyes from filling with tears.

Dora Puts the Kettle On

"Motherhood is the basket in which you have placed all your eggs," she said softly when she saw my wet cheek. She gave me a hug, then went to answer the call of the whistling teakettle.

~

Charlotte Mason's students used watercolor paints to make their pictures. Art supply stores supply quality paints and brushes. Would your children enjoy experimenting with watercolors?

~

In what way does keeping a Nature Notebook follow the "gentle art of learning?"

~

What did Dora mean when she told Carol, "Motherhood is the basket in which you have placed all your eggs?"

Tomorrow We Go Home

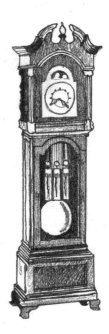

I t's been a comfort to me that Bob reads to the children each evening. It's enabled me keep up my diary. All is quiet now. As I write I can hear him downstairs winding up the grandfather clock. It is the last thing he does every night before getting into bed. I also hear the plink-plink of Reliable's long claws on the wooden floor as he follows his master. Earlier I was sitting alone with my private thoughts, with nothing to distract me. Worry beset me. It crept upon me. What news will Michael have about his job when I return? Why can't conflicts be resolved? Will he get so fed up that he will have to quit? No, he would never do that. He seems to be so suited for his job. To stop myself, I wrapped my shawl around my shoulders more tightly and stood in the doorway of the children's bedroom, brooding over them while they slept. I sometimes do this at home when Michael works late. It gives me comfort and it's easier to pray for them this way. This is what I did tonight. Silvery blue moon-light cast a soft glow on their faces. How peaceful they looked. It seems not too long ago that each evening I had to pull Emily's thumb out of her mouth once she had fallen asleep, to discourage her from sucking it during the night. Don no longer sleeps with his Teddy, but of late he has kept a hodgepodge of rocks and pebbles on his nightstand. Here at Bob's there is a token rock by his bedside — pink granite, it looks like.

I want to look pretty for Michael tomorrow and so I'm going to bed with rag curls in my hair. I'm far too tired to write anything else tonight.

$\sim$

What kinds of rocks can be scavenged from your neighborhood?

Marvelous
Snowflakes

Reliable nosed his way around the corner of the barn when he heard the pickup truck start, making an imploring whimper and wagging his tail hopefully. Ordinarily, this entreaty might win him a ride in the truck, but today it was utterly packed full of potatoes, suitcases, and four human beings. Bob, Don, Emily, and myself were on our way to the city. Inside Don's suitcase was the copy of *Swiss Family Robinson* his uncle had let him borrow. I had my old Nature Notebook and the new hat Dora had given me. I had also tucked away Bob's morning compliment about how nice I looked. Both children were returning home with Notebooks full of new drawings and writing.

There was still snow along the lane. The sky was gray. As we passed the maples the children listened as their uncle told them about maple sugar making. He explained how

Chapter
28

each year in late February and early March he collects the sap in buckets that he checks every day. He stokes up a fire to keep the sap evaporating — just as my father did, I remembered. The mud can be deep and glutinous, but the oxen do an excellent job of dragging a wooden sled through it to transport the sap buckets.

"I wonder who planted these trees so many years ago," I said. "Did Dad ever tell you?"

"No, but whoever it was believed in the principle, 'Plant a pear for an heir.' I think the people of America today are drifting away from this. Don't you?" Bob was referring to Daniel Webster's advice to younger farmers: "Plant trees, adorn your grounds, live for the benefit of those who shall come after you."[1] This would have been perfect timing for Bob to compare the work ethic of those in the city (making a quick buck with big profit) to those in the country (making an honest living from the land). However, Bob's graciousness and polite self-control prevented him from doing so. He is a true country gentleman. How is it, though, that I always seem to be thinking exactly what he *would* say?

~

"Goodbye Uncle Bob!" the children sang out when, having arrived in front of our bungalow, they happily tumbled out of the truck. Bob unloaded our suitcases from the back of the truck, set them down before the front door, and gave them each a bear hug.

"Goodbye, Sis. See you!" he said, planting a bristly kiss on my cheek.

There were no lessons today due to our traveling and the fact that there were dishes left in the sink, clothes to wash, and bags to unpack. Michael had managed to wash some clothes and hang them up on the lines in the basement. Everyone in the house was occupied this gray afternoon. Immediately upon entering his room, Don became absorbed in his tinker toys. Emily filled the bird feeder and took out her paper dolls. Unnoticed, the snow began to softly fall. When we finally noticed it, everything outside was completely covered with a layer of white. I said a prayer that Bob would make it home safely.

When Don saw the snowflakes fall, he said, "I'm sick of snow."

Marvelous Snowflakes

Emily, looking out of the window at the mention of snow, burst out, "Mother, look at the red bird!"

"Come quick, Don, look at the beautiful male cardinal!" I called. I had seen cardinals plenty of times before but, because I was sharing the experience with the children, this time there was a newness to it. Don and Emily both stood looking out the window at the feeder. "This bird wouldn't look half so beautiful if there weren't white snow behind it to show it off," I said. "There's the female. Do you see her? She's mostly tawny, not as red as the mate is, but she is pretty, too." The scene was as pretty as a Christmas card.

We were watching the pair of birds so intently that we didn't hear Michael's car pull up. He must have seen our three heads silhouetted in the lighted window, because he walked onto the porch to greet us. When his grinning face suddenly appeared at the window, we were all startled.

"Boo!" he said in reaction to the surprised looks on our faces. Once inside, the children hung on him excitedly. He freed himself by saying he had a little present for them to share between them, and reached into his briefcase for it.

"Open it," he said, adding that they were to share it. Don unwrapped the package. "It's a magnifying glass!" he announced. "Thank you."

"May I see it?" asked Emily.

"Just a minute," said Don. Michael took that opportunity to give me a long embrace. He told me he had missed me so.

For dinner I had put together a soup — of sorts — from my store of canned goods and the scraps of food I had found about the place. Michael said it was much more satisfying than anything he had put together for himself over the past two weeks. He admitted to having become rather familiar with the man at the hot dog stand, the pretzel stand, and the corner diner, partly out of hunger and partly out of loneliness.

"I'm sick of snow," Don complained again. I had to rebuke him. His clever dad came to the rescue. "Have you ever seen a snowflake really close up?" he asked.

"Nope."

"Well, you can use the magnifying glass to see them. And you won't find any two alike. They're all different. Tonight's gentle snowfall will give you nice unbroken ones."

Marvelous Snowflakes

I found a piece of black cloth from my scrap bag.

"Isn't it too dark outside?" asked Don. I put the two parlor lamps in the porch window. When the snowflakes were caught, the porch light and the light from the window were enough to provide a good look. Under Michael's direction Don and Emily took turns catching snowflakes and using their new magnifying glass. I stood on the porch steps, shivering. "What do you see?" asked Michael, pulling up his collar and tying his scarf to ward off the cold. The children went on to describe the snow crystals — each with six sides and yet each decorated a little differently. This activity held their interest for quite some time so that they unknowingly missed their radio show. Michael spoke to them of a Mr. W. A. Bentley who set about photographing thousands of snowflakes.[2]

~

Emily was leaning against her father. His arm on her shoulder must have felt heavy but probably gave her a secure feeling. When it was her turn to use the glass, without moving from her comfortable spot, she chose the ones that had landed on her dad's black coat sleeve. "They're lovely," she said sweetly in her little voice. We could tell she was tired, so we ushered them both indoors to get ready for bed. I was encouraged that Don's attitude toward snow had changed — at least for the time being. And although we did not do formal lessons today, I am reassured that the children did learn something new — first from Bob's maple syrup story, next from the visit of the cardinals, and then from a close-up view of God's gorgeous snowflakes. It was a full day. But perhaps not full enough. I have a list of troubling questions I wish to ask Michael when the time is right.

~

Cardinal — Cardinalis cardinalis
Sugar maples — Acer saccharum

~

Marvelous Snowflakes

Explain the phrase, "Plant a pear for an heir."

~

Wilson Bently (1865-1931) was homeschooled until he started high school. Examine a snowflake during the next snowfall or check out Mr. Bently's collection of photographs — taken in the 1920's — in his book, Snow Crystals.

Michael's Speech

I couldn't wait for any "right time." I was impatient. Last night, after the children were asleep and we were retiring, I let the words slip out. Anxiety has a way of making one lose one's self-control. Michael was hanging up his tie behind the bedroom closet door when I came out with it. Because he is normally uncommunicative, especially when it comes to his work, I was surprised to receive an all-out speech.

"Carol, I wish I could tell you everything is going to be all right, but I can't," he told me. He went on to answer some of my troublesome questions about the company. This is the gist of what he said as I remember it: "You see, the big guys make the money decisions. They like to spend it, allocate it, and play with it. They boss around the little guys who must show loyal dedication by working late, if necessary, at trying to *make* the money. When the big guys

Chapter
29

Michael's Speech

make mistakes they just push the little guys to keep coming up with new ways of making *more* money. When a little guy like me has a good idea they get the credit for it. When the little guys can't come up with innovative ideas fast enough or efficiently enough, the big guys get nervous and so they lean harder on the little guys... or fire them. And if a little guy with no talent wants to work his way up in the company, he flatters with platitudes and does whatever it takes just short of hard work. Sometimes clever, ambitious types who aspire to get ahead too quickly are a threat to the big guys. To get rid of this threat, the big guys fire them, too. I've tried to stay in the middle — not too high-powered but capable of coming up with some good ideas. It's a balancing act. And I feel as though I'm destined to mediocrity. The whole thing is a game. Most of the time I can go on working in my office without things bothering me, but at other times the whole thing disgusts me."

Michael's tale was not a comforting one but I found it satisfying to know more about his life at the office. I tried to respond with hopefulness, yet the anxiety in my tone must have been evident. "But you're good at what you do, your boss told you so," I said.

"Yes, *J* think I am." Then he held both my hands firmly in his and looked me straight in the eyes. "You really shouldn't worry about it," he told me. Brief though it was, it was a command and he was serious. He knows how an anxious woman can affect the home atmosphere. His own mother was a worrier.

"You've been taking time with Don and Emily to consider the flowers of the field and the birds of the air. How is it that you've missed the important point of that message?" I knew what Christ's message was, and felt a pang of conviction. Because he is a gentleman it is not Michael's way to prolong a moment of admonishment. Turning my hands about in his he said, "You've been working hard, too. I can tell. You're probably overspent. But you know you'll always be my sweetheart. I'm so glad you're home," he whispered, as he held me close.

That was last night. This morning something in my reading jumped out at me. This paragraph by Henry D. Thoreau so marvelously illustrates Michael's admonishment from Mathew 6:30 that I am recording it here in my diary:

Michael's Speech

I saw a delicate flower had grown up two feet high, between the horses' path and the wheeltrack. An inch more to right or left had sealed its fate, or an inch higher; and yet it lived to flourish as much as if it had a thousand acres of untrodden space around it, and never knew the danger it incurred. It did not borrow trouble, nor invite an evil fate by apprehending it.[1]

~

I am resolved to trust and obey, as it says in the hymn, for there is no other way to be happy in Jesus and have a happy marriage.

~

Why did Christ Jesus bid us to consider the lilies of the field and the birds of the air?

Spring

Thank You for the Birds that Sing

March 1936

The robins are back. I awoke to their twitterings and the sound of the soft spring rain. You can't keep a robin down. He sings in the rain and is always cheerful. If only I could be more like that. I recall reading that it is the males that return first. A week or two later the females arrive and the business of home-building begins. So I guess it was a male robin that sang loudly and distinctly just outside my bedroom window. Its voice rises above the chorus of the other birds as the notes of a tenor soloist rise above the others in an opera. "Cheerily cheer-up cheerio" — his song calls me out of winter's bleak days. I parted the curtains. It is good to be

Chapter
30

able to open the windows. The spring thaw has brought earthworms to the surface. On the sidewalk below was the songster, slurping up his earthworm just the way some people slurp up spaghetti. Earthworms would make another good Nature Study.

Clumps of dark green grass-like leaves poke up out of the wet ground on either side of the front walk. In the center of each clump is a purple bud. The crocuses are making their spring début.

Although the morning was overcast, all the gloominess that can creep into a winter's day has passed with the arrival of spring. The sun, now rising above the horizon with more eagerness and sinking below it with more reluctance, sends out its lingering rays to wake the sleepy world from its dormancy. Because of the chilly drizzle the children stayed indoors after lessons but they were entertained by the robins and were quite glad at having spotted the crocuses — asking to see if I had made an entry of either in my childhood Nature Notebook. There is a verse in my old Notebook that Emily wanted to copy into hers. It is from "A Bird" by Emily Dickinson:

A bird came down the walk:
He did not know I saw;
He bit an angleworm in halves
And ate the fellow, raw.

And then he drank a dew
From a convenient grass,
And then hopped sidewise to the wall
To let a beetle pass.

~

In the evening when it was dark and the children were already tucked in bed for the night, a strange noise impelled them to venture out of their room. Michael and I were downstairs in the kitchen. He had come home late from work and I was serving him the supper I had set aside for him. We recognized the usual pitter-patter of feet. "Hey you two, I thought you were in bed," I heard him say, as I followed him up the stairs. Emily, standing in the hall, pointed to the window as we reached the landing. A moment later we were all staring at a full moon, watching shadowy figures fly across it.

"Oh, it was the honking of the wild geese that..." Michael stopped, took one step closer to the window and said, more quietly, "Aren't they spectacular?" Yes, they were spectacular, with the moonlight on their wings.

"Where are they going?" asked Emily.

Her dad answered, "I don't know exactly. But I do know they're headed back up north," I had gone downstairs to finish the washing up while Michael tucked them back into bed. He confessed to me later that although he was glad Emily had a bubbling curiosity, he was not able to answer any of her questions concerning the habits of migrating birds. "I just told her that it is a wonder how geese can travel so far without a map," he said. It seems early for Canadian geese. Maybe this means a warm spring. I think tomorrow I shall visit the library for a picture book on geese and look up the chapter on geese in Comstock's *Handbook*.

⌇

American robin — Turdus migratorius
Canada goose — Branta canadensis
Crocus — Crocus vernus
Earthworms ("night crawlers") — Lumbricus

⌇

Have you ever noticed a flock of birds in the sky? Which birds live in your area only at certain times of the year?

Seed Catalog

April 1936

J ust as the children and I stepped out the kitchen door for a sunny afternoon walk to the library, Bob pulled into the driveway. He hasn't come for over a month, due to the difficulty of driving on country roads in mud season. No doubt he had a backlog of chores in town, because instead of getting out of the truck as he normally would, he put his arm out of the truck window and held out a quart jar full of maple syrup.

"Thanks Uncle Bob!" said Don. Bob handed a second to Emily and a third to me. We echoed, "Thanks, Uncle Bob!"

"You're welcome," he called over the noise of the truck's idling engine. Then, with judicial emphasis, "Hold them carefully. Ten gallons of sap went into each of those jars." I exchanged a few words with him, inquiring about Dora and the state of the farm, answering yes to his fervent request that we come visit on Easter. Michael was needed

Chapter
31

to sing a part in the church quartet, he added. Then he was off, leaving us standing in a cloud of unpleasant exhaust fumes as we waved goodbye.

"What's that, Mother?" asked Emily, when the cloud cleared.

"Oh, this? It looks like Uncle Bob's seed catalog."

"May I see it?"

"We'll look at it together when we get back." The jars were carefully stowed on a shelf in the cellar and we too were off.

~

On the way home from the library I wasn't sure I really wanted to make the detour through the park because my shopping bag full of library books was very heavy. I was also a little queasy in the stomach. But the children urged me, and I agreed — on the condition that they would add another entry to their Nature Notebooks.

Tender green sprouts were pushing up through the grass as well as through the mulch under the trees. Parts of the lawn seldom walked on were speckled with tiny pale blue flowers. Emily kneeled down to examine them. I didn't know their name until today, when I checked my field guide and read that they are bluets. These dainty bluets have stems half an inch long with leaves no larger than a grain of rice. The wee blooms are perfect in form and matchlessly blue in coloring, too tiny to pick or to put into bouquets. The children took turns looking at them through their magnifying glass. Perhaps Mr. Murphy will let the bluets bloom a week or two longer before he mows.

None of the trees have their leaves out yet but the red maples were in flower. I reached up and bent a branch down so the children could see the flowers close up. "Did you know trees have flowers? See the tiny red blossoms?" I asked them. "Sugar maples have green ones." We used the magnifying glass on these tiny flowers and on the blossoms of the oak tree catkins.

On the walk home I recognized the narrow leaves of the daffodils sprouting everywhere. This is the flower I most look forward to. I know just where to expect them around the neighborhood. It won't be long now. I remember my mother telling me that the leaves of the daffodil are the season's directives to begin spring sewing. By the time the yellowing buds of the daffodils were ready to open she had finished sewing my new dress for Easter and was well into the task of making a few play clothes for me. Now it is my turn to be the seamstress. I wonder how I will fit sewing into my already full schedule.

I hastened the children's pace because I was feeling queasier in the stomach. Even so, upon returning home I had to pause before entering the house. I spotted a pair of robins building a nest in a tree in our front yard. We stood there for some minutes watching them. What a lovely sight! Once indoors I piled the library books on Don's desk — a little sloppily — and went upstairs for a lie-down. Don and Emily had some milk and brought up a glass to me. They were sprawled on my bedroom rug, quietly scanning the pages of the seed catalog — pointing to the plants and vegetables they recognized. "Mmm, I want to plant melons," said Don stoutly, "and pumpkins."

"I'd like to plant strawberries. I love straw-ber-ries," said Emily drawing out the word strawberry for emphasis.

"May we plant them in the backyard, Mother?"

I was not sharing any of their excitement. I felt like a kill-joy at first but I managed to end optimistically. "Our backyard is barely big enough to hang the wash," I said, "let alone accommodate melons and pumpkins. And with all the strawberries grown up the hill from Uncle Bob's, we don't need to grow them ourselves. Strawberries take a couple of years to mature anyway. And our soil is poor. Let me see the catalog, please," I said suddenly. My suspicions were raised again. Why did my brother give me his catalog when he had finished ordering from it? I saw the pencil marks he had made. He hadn't ever shared his catalog before. But as soon as my eyes landed on the sunflowers, I began to daydream — of a backyard filled with hot yellow sunshine and my mother's bright yellow flowers, humming with bees and all aflutter with butterflies. I remembered, too, running through meadows of yellow flowers. "I know what we can plant," I said, the sunny scene still in my head.

"What?" asked Don and Emily in unison.

"Sunflowers. They grow in poor soil and they grow up, not out. Let's get these tall ones right here." The children, looking over my shoulder, agreed.

"How tall?"

Seed Catalog

"They grow as tall as Dad, or taller."

"Really?"

"Really. Now let me rest and I'll be down to cook supper soon." I left my milk untouched. I don't know why, but I'm not ready to tell Michael that I'm going to have another baby. I have so wanted another child. Maybe the reason is that I'd like things to be better for him at work first. But who knows how long that will be. A career that involves carrying a psychological burden along with a heavy briefcase may not be so terrific after all.

~

Bluet — Houstonia caerulea
Sunflower — Helianthus annuus

~

Do you have room to grow a new plant? How about starting it from seed? Everyone has room for a windowsill garden.

~

Come spring, what tender green sprouts are to be found in your neighborhood?

~

Have you ever looked close up at a tree flower?

Canary Cage

It is Saturday night and Michael is continuing the reading of Bob's *Swiss Family Robinson* to the children. It is a long story to read aloud but they are nearly finished. What a day it has been! I was busy at the sewing machine, trying to ignore my incessant nausea. Don went out to play with George, a neighbor boy. In the driveway I could hear Emily playing hopscotch with George's sister, Pam, a girl a few years older than Emily. They were so nicely occupied. It took some time to chalk the squares and numbers and for each of them to find just the right flat stone. I thought, then, that they were seriously underway. But it wasn't long before I heard Emily say, "I'd rather roller skate." And then she was in the kitchen, asking me where her skates were. I found them on the front porch and was retrieving them when I heard George tell Don, "Hey, there's a nest in that tree."

Canary Cage

"Yes, I know. We watched it being built," Don told him.

George picked up a hopscotch stone, put it in his slingshot, and aimed at a robin. "Hey, don't do that!" cried Don. George was probably just trying to kid. He really isn't a bad boy. But when he let the stone go it hit the female robin in the wing. Alarmed, it began flapping lopsidedly in a circle in the grass, unable to fly. "That's it, George," Don said indignantly, "I'm not playing with you anymore today." George forced a laugh, but I could tell he really was sorry. When I stood up and he saw me, he and Pam ran home. Emily, too, had seen what happened, and cried out, "Georgie-Porgie, nasty boy!" I was surprised to hear such a loud cry from my quiet little girl.

"You're right, Emily, that was a nasty thing to do, but don't name-call. He's probably feeling bad about it."

I didn't know what to do. We just stood there watching it flutter helplessly. But as we tip-toed over to inspect the bird, Mr. Thurston, from across the street, came over and, as we watched, bound a splint to the injured wing. He must have been sitting on his front porch watching the whole scene. He had brought with him an old canary cage for the robin's safe convalescence.

"Do you have a cup hook you can screw into the ceiling of your porch? I can hang the cage up there near the nest, away from cats," he said. I got the cup hook, wondering what would become of the eggs.

The children came inside and watched from the front window. Amazingly, father robin rose to the emergency. He took his mate's place on the eggs, and brooded them very carefully. It had been his habit to bring worms to his mate so that she need never leave the nest, but now he had to steal away and hustle his own food, being careful to get back before the eggs were chilled. Even with this double task in hand, however, he insisted on feeding his wounded mate. He brought her many juicy worms, pushing his beak through the bars to meet hers.

As soon as Michael returned with packages from the market, the children explained the dramatic incident to him, pulling him by his arms to the front window. We all watched father robin. On his front porch across the street Mr. Thurston was watching, too. After some minutes Don's mind made an association. He blurted out, "Hey, now father robin will have to work as much as Dad."

Spring

Canary Cage

Michael's shoulders drooped. I put my arm around him, trying to be comforting. He is so good at not verbalizing complaints about his work, but I could tell by the piercing glance he gave me that there was one on the tip of his tongue that very moment.

~

Have you ever watched a bird build a nest? Keep your eyes open in early spring. Lay some pieces of yarn over a bush to give the birds a supply of nest-building materials.

Not a Sparrow Falls

Don usually whizzes through his arithmetic, but this morning both he and Emily had a difficult time concentrating. When I commented on their daydreaming, their excuse was that they wanted to hear if father or mother robin would resume singing. Both had been quiet — mother robin because she was hurt, father robin because he was preoccupied and perhaps too exhausted to sing. Nipping their lack of attention in the bud, I said, "If you want to hear a robin sing, you'll have to listen for their song much earlier in the morning. Listen at your bedroom window before coming down for breakfast. Right now you need to get back to your numbers." After arithmetic was completed I listened to Emily read aloud. I am happy with her improvement. It seems long ago now that reading was such a struggle for her. Daily patience and attentive interest on my part, joined with

Chapter
33

Spring
~125~

consistent effort on hers, has led to very satisfying progress. Then it was Don's turn to read aloud. He does well reading silently, but I still give him practice in reading aloud from time to time, especially the reading of poetry.[H]

As a break between lessons, I had Emily stand on the kitchen stool to try on her new dress. I was pinning up the hem just as Michael walked into the kitchen. Everyone was surprised to see him. He greeted us with a strained cheerfulness. I saw through his attempt at his usual calm deportment and asked, "Are you not well?"

"Something like that. Carol, I need to talk to you."

"Um... children go upstairs, read a chapter of one of your books, and then you can be finished with lessons for the day. Emily, change out of your new dress — careful of the pins — and lay it on my bed." They obeyed promptly and without questions, sensing the tension in the air.

"What is it?" I asked, steadying my nerves by randomly repositioning the pins in my pincushion.

Michael's head lowered and he confessed, "I lost my job."

I pushed the pincushion aside and folded my hands together on the table as if in prayer. My wifely intuition had whispered to me that this news was inevitable, so I wasn't surprised. "Oh honey, I'm sorry," I said as gently and as hopefully as I could. I didn't question him because he didn't seem to want to talk about it. After a tense minute or two of silence, I faced the direction of the front porch and remarked, "I've been watching the robins, and I know God will take care of us."

"I was praying all the way home that you'd take it that way," he admitted, greatly relieved. And he took my hands in his. "I'll look for new work in the morning." That was that. There was nothing more either of us wanted to say about the matter. He wore a small peaceful smile and so did I. Each was the kind of sincere, purposeful smile — supernaturally bestowed from above, I believe — that had the power to uplift a friend in need. Then it occurred to me that there was something *I* wanted to share with *him*, but I decided it could wait a few more days... or weeks. In the midst of my secret deliberating, the children called excitedly from the top of the stairs.

"Mother! Dad! Listen, father robin is singing!"

⌒

Which birds can you identify by their songs?

⌒

Can you recall the words to the hymn "His Eye is On the Sparrow?" What do they mean to you?

When Daffodils Begin to Peer

I haven't written in awhile because I've been spending more time with my prayer journal. This morning it was strange not to wake up to the clicking of the typewriter. Every workday for almost two weeks Michael had risen early to type letters to prospective employers. He then followed up contacts in the afternoons. Since all these efforts proved fruitless, last night we decided to break this monotonous disheartening routine and leave for our Easter vacation with Bob and Dora a few days earlier than we had planned. Mr. Thurston, who is looking after Don's goldfish, assured Don that he would also keep an eye on the robins. The car was packed with suitcases, hatboxes, a couple of field guides, and (I remembered) Emily's needy cardigan. Uncle Bob's copy of *Swiss Family Robinson* was being returned.

As is my custom, before getting into the car I scanned the sky for various signs of weather. On this windy after-

Chapter

34

Spring
~128~

noon the blue sky was covered with puffs of white clouds that looked like sheep roaming from east to west. Sheep and family were headed in the same direction!

From my window I saw daffodils beginning to bloom in nearly every yard! "When daffodils begin to peer... Why, then comes in the sweet o' the year..."[1] I said, quoting Shakespeare.

"Oh, is that what that yellow flower is called?" asked Michael. Don laughed, because he thought his dad was kidding. But the truth is, since he's been out of work, he's had much more time to observe the world around him and he is learning the names of things he hasn't before paid much attention to. Once we were past all the traffic signals it was smooth sailing through the countryside.

The open fields were wearing their new spring grass of yellow-green, dotted with dabs of yellow dandelions that were still so short they didn't look like weeds. Each hayfield, framed by its rough stone walls, appeared to be one big French impressionistic painting after another. When Michael slowed down to go through the village of Appleton, he noticed that at the edge of the street in front of the church there were hordes of daffodils — all nodding their heads up and down in the wind.

"My word! Take a look at all those daffodils," he remarked casually, as though he had always known what daffodils looked like. My normally quiet husband was unusually perky.

~

When Aunt Dora told the children that a calf had been born since their last visit, they raced out through the mudroom door for the barn. Then I got to hold Jonathan who, with his round curls, round face, and round eyes, looks just like one of Raphael's winged cherubs.

"Has Michael found any work?" asked Dora.

"He's been looking but he hasn't found anything like what he was doing. He said that it is much easier to land a new job when you already have one. But our lease is up in a couple months and..."

"And?"

Because I was brought up to keep one's money problems and expenses to oneself, I didn't tell her that Michael and I would be using

some of our savings to pay next month's rent. Changing the subject, I said, "I wonder... how do you think sunflowers would look between my kitchen door and our driveway?"

~

Dora remained in the kitchen to add more wood to the woodstove and check on her pot of baked beans while I wandered out toward the barn. In the distance I saw Bob and Michael standing near the garden shed. Bob, spade in one hand, was communicating something passionately, making gesticulations with the other hand. Michael, arms crossed, listened conscientiously. How strange! My brother isn't usually so animated. Then it was Bob who listened and Michael who made the gesticulations. Oh, if I could only hear what it was all about! But the wind carried their voices away. Bob was supposed be searching for early signs of asparagus sprouts for Dora.

I found my two children in the barn. Emily took me to see the calf. "Isn't she lovely?" she said, stroking its head. Don was swinging wildly on the rope.

"Would you like to take a walk with me to my old secret spot in the woods?" I asked. I had their clipboards, a field guide, and the magnifying glass with me, so they knew what I was up to. We walked across the pasture and toward the same evergreen woods where we had once collected pinecones. Beyond the evergreens was a forest of aspens, birches, oaks, maples, and ash. The deciduous trees seemed ready and waiting for the right hour to put forth their leaves, but it wasn't the trees I was interested in today — it was the forest floor. As we stepped upon the moist springy carpet of decaying leaves and pine needles, we detected their sweet musky aroma. At the edge of the woods Don was first to spot a deep red trillium growing in the dappled sunlight.

"'*Tri*' is Latin for three," I told them. I pointed out the plant's three leaves, three sepals, and three petals. Emily smelled the flower but declared it to be "nasty." The trillium was solitary. We could find no others. Both Don and Emily sat on a nearby rock to draw it. I had brought colored pencils with me so they could finish their drawings right there in the woods. Nearby, there was another plant, which had an arching stem with small greenish white bells hanging along it. I recognized it from my childhood, but had to flip through the field guide to learn its name: Solomon's seal. I had the children draw one of these, too. The ferns are uncurling their fronds like fiddleheads. Don forced one to uncurl but it rolled back up again.

Leaves the size of kitten's ears were sprouting up through the dry leaves. "What are these, Mom?" asked Don. "They're all over the place."

I told him they were mayflowers or wild lily-of-the-valley. "They will bloom at the same time that garden lily-of-the-valley blooms. Next month they'll have fuzzy white flowers. In September there'll be berries on them," I explained as we walked. It's strange that such a flourishing plant has only one leaf.

We heard a *Fee-bee!* "That's the chickadee's spring song," I told them. "Listen!" Its glad tidings accompanied us on our walk but,

When Daffodils Begin to Peer

although we looked above us, around us, and through the branches of the trees, the happy bird was evasive — invisible. With this fairy bird seemingly leading the way with its *fee-bees*, we walked deeper into the woods and came to the place where I used to sit all by myself.

It's a clearing with a large flat ledge of rock covered with lichen and in the puddles of the rocky surface grows moss. It is a still, private place that is surrounded with trees that block all breezes. Ah, tranquility — everyone needs a little of it. Remembering that Christ went into a garden to pray, I was steeped in a sense of sanctuary. A peaceful feeling, the kind that can soothe away the rush and noise of life, encircled me like the trees encircled the secret spot. At last my practical side reasserted itself and I opened my field guide. "Let's see, according to the guide, this moss is called hair-cap moss or goldilocks. Can you think why it's called goldilocks, Emily?"

"It has gold hair growing out of all the green," she said, running her hand over the thick carpet. We peeked through the magnifying glass at the lichen and the moss. Then Emily looked all around her and said, "This is like the place where Bambi was born." Apparently the story was still fresh in her memory, though we had finished reading it months ago.

"Yes it is," I agreed. And as I explored the secluded haven further, I commented, "It's just the right kind of place for deer to rest, and I think those droppings over there prove it," I said, indicating several piles of pellets among the moss. Don, who had been sitting on some spongy moss, automatically stood up. His breeches were damp, but he didn't mind because he hadn't found what he was looking for where he had been sitting.

Then my rock collector picked up a small stone. One corner of it was pointed — the rest was like a smooth handle. Therefore, to Don's delight, it had all the attributes of a scraping tool. He tried out his stone, scraping away some moss. "Hey, what's this?" Don exclaimed, brushing off an area of the step now free of moss. "There's something written here!" After more brushing with the palm of his hand, he read "Carol 1915."

"That's you, Mom, isn't it?" he asked excitedly.

A glimmer of a recollection came to my mind. "Yes, I did that a long time ago. Why don't you and Emily add your names to this secret spot?" They thought it was a fine idea. But before they could get started, I said, "Isn't that the dinner bell?"

"Yup and I'm hungry," Don responded. It was faint but it was irrefutably Dora's dinner bell.

~

This seems to be the day for uncovering things. At twilight when I was walking down the upstairs hall, I noticed a stray piece of paper sticking out from under the closet door. Impulsively I reached down to pull it through. It ripped. When I saw that the writing on it was in my mother's hand, I was upset that I had been so hasty. Haste makes waste for sure. I opened the door to find the other half under the box from whence came my Nature Notebook. When I put the two little halves together I found a poem by John Newton, the author of "Amazing Grace," copied out in my mother's careful handwriting. I am copying the words in my diary because I believe them to have brought my mother hope and comfort at the end of a long dark winter:

> *Kindly spring again is here,*
> *Trees and fields in bloom appear;*
> *Hark! The birds with artless lays*
> *Warble their creator's praise.*

> *Where in winter all was snow,*
> *Now the flowers in clusters grow;*
> *And the corn, in green array,*
> *Promises a harvest-day.*

When Daffodils Begin to Peer

Lord, afford a spring to me,
Let me feel like what I see;
Speak, and by thy gracious voice,
Make my drooping soul rejoice.

On the garden deign to smile,
Raise the plants, enrich the soil;
Soon thy presence will restore
Life to what seemed dead before.

~

Black-capped chickadee — Parus atricapillus
Christmas fern — Polystichum arostichoides
Daffodils — Narcissus
Haircap moss — Polytrichum juniperinum
Mayflower ("wild lily-of-the-valley") — Maianthemum canadense
Northern maidenhair fern — Adiantum pedatum
Red trillium — Trillium erectum
Ring lichen — Arctoparmelia centrifuga
Sensitive fern — Onoclea sensibilis
Solomon's seal — Polygonatum pubescens

~

Are there any shady places where you can examine
non-flowering plants such as lichen, fern or moss?

Balm of Gilead

T he old piano bench creaked under Bob's weight, signaling to all the men that it was time to begin rehearsal. The children and I were seated in the parlor to hear the singing. Pastor, Bob, Michael, and a Mr. Pease form the quartet. Mr. Pease is seventy-four years young. I say "young" because Dora told me he still keeps a big garden plot, gets up his own wood, plays merrily on the church organ, and tends the cemetery. I am so glad Michael was asked to be part of a team of men who publicly testify to Christ's glorious resurrection. Ministering to others is a way to lift one's mind away from one's own problems. It was a balm to me to hear their voices blending in praise.

When rehearsal was over, Bob announced, "And now there is a song I'd like to play for Auntie Carol." With another creak of the old piano bench, he began playing

Balm of Gilead

and singing "This Is My Father's World." What a perfect hymn for spring-time! This hymn, for me, marks the beginning of Michael's greater appreciation of the natural world around him and a desire to know it more intimately. I prayed silently right there in the parlor that nature would become a welcome distraction from our pressing problems and concerns — and that we would take time to be grateful for it.

This is my Father's world, And to my listening ears
All nature sings, and round me rings, The music of the spheres.
This is my Father's world: I rest me in the thought
Of rocks and trees, of skies and seas — His hand the wonders
wrought.

This is my Father's world, The birds their carols raise,
The morning light, the lily white, Declare their Maker's praise.
This is my Father's world: He shines in all that's fair;
In the rustling grass I hear him pass, He speaks to me everywhere.

This is my Father's world, O let me ne'er forget
That though the wrong seems oft so strong, God is the Ruler yet.
This is my Father's world: The battle is not done;
Jesus who died shall be satisfied, And earth and heaven be one.

~

Life can be stressful. What a comfort it is to "rest me in the thought" that God is ruling, that Christ is sustaining all things by his powerful Word. Have you comforted yourself with such thoughts lately?

Uncle Bob Takes Care

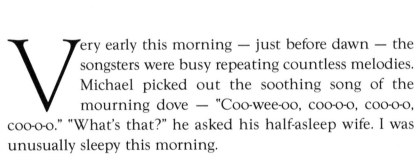

Very early this morning — just before dawn — the songsters were busy repeating countless melodies. Michael picked out the soothing song of the mourning dove — "Coo-wee-oo, coo-o-o, coo-o-o, coo-o-o." "What's that?" he asked his half-asleep wife. I was unusually sleepy this morning.

"Mmm?"

"What bird is that?" It repeated its song.

"A mourning dove," is all I said, and turned over, dreading another day of nausea.

"A mourning dove," he murmured to himself.

He gave a "Good morning" to his wide-awake children. "Hey, did you hear the mourning dove?"

"Yup," they said simply.

I hadn't expected last night's prayer in the parlor to be answered so soon and so early.

Chapter
36

Spring

Uncle Bob Takes Care

After breakfast I was helping Dora make cakes for Easter Sunday as well as some other dishes. Dora was expecting more guests for Sunday dinner. The children had left the kitchen long ago. "We need more eggs," I stated. Michael volunteered to find our pair of egg collectors. "Let's go together," I said.

We searched around the barnyard but they weren't anywhere in sight, so we collected the eggs ourselves. Michael insisted on carrying the full basket back to the house and just as I was thinking to myself how silly he looked, we saw the children running across the field and through the barnyard toward us. "The groundhogs, Mom! Mom, the groundhogs are up!" they announced breathlessly.

"What? Ho! Watch you don't knock the eggs," Michael said, as Don grabbed his father's arm. Since Michael had never entered a poultry house to collect eggs before, he was not about to be thwarted in his first daring attempt.

"Oh, they are?" I responded, pondering. I thought to myself, "I'd better tell your Uncle Bob about this when he returns from delivering the milk."

Back in the kitchen, Dora was quiet when she heard the news, but concern filled her large eyes.

"Dad, will you come with us to see them?" asked Don.

"There's fifty of them!" Emily informed us, but was quickly corrected by Don.

"About twelve," was Don's more accurate report.

"Sure, show me the way," their dad said.

Only a quarter of an hour later, Bob and I joined them in the pasture.

"Aren't they cute, Uncle Bob?" asked Emily.

Bob gave a weak "Yup" and his eyes narrowed. Emily didn't see Bob's well-polished European shotgun that was hanging off the back of his shoulder. "I don't know where these varmints have come from. We've never had so many before."

"Children, come back to the house with your dad and me."

"Why?" they asked, together.

"Just come back to the house. Aunt Dora might need us to look for more eggs." We took Reliable with us, too. We started walking but Emily turned around to look behind her and saw the shotgun. "No, Daddy," she moaned, but kept walking. It seemed like a long walk and before we got to the door we heard "Pop, pop, pop" more times than anyone wished to count. "Pop goes the weasel," my father would say whenever he returned from having to shoot something. Emily burst into the kitchen and ran upstairs. "I'll talk to her," I said. I took a deep breath and prayed for words of wisdom. I found her on the bed with her head buried under the pillow.

"Your Uncle Bob is a man who takes care," I explained to her. "He takes care of Aunt Dora and Jonathan, he takes care of Reliable, Rubarb, his oxen, his fields, his garden, his barn of cows... he takes care of the whole farm! Shooting the groundhogs is one way he takes care of his cows. If a cow gets its leg caught in a groundhog hole, it could break a leg. Uncle Bob depends on his cows." I answered some of her questions and then suggested that she go back downstairs to dye eggs with Dora. Dora is as good at dyeing eggs as she is at dyeing wool. I remained sitting on Emily's bed a minute longer, thinking about something that Dora had told me. My brother leaves milk at the doors of families who can't pay him. He does a lot of taking care. And then it occurred to me that he looks after me, too. As I descended the stairs I was met with another thought: Patrick Murphy's live traps each filled with a plump ground-hog... hand delivered to the countryside.

~

Mourning dove — Zenaida macroura

~

We are to be wise caretakers of the earth. In some countries it is unlawful or irreligious to kill a rat. What is your opinion on the matter?

Easter Sunday

On this bright Easter morning Emily pointed out to me the ladybug crawling on her window — another creature waking from its winter dormancy. And I can verify that the climate of this upstairs in winter is just right for hibernation. After watching it a bit we opened the window and let it "fly away home," as the nursery rhyme strongly recommends.

The Easter eggs were hidden all over the kitchen and parlor. The children delighted in finding them. Afterwards we donned our Sunday best. I think Emily looked as cute as a Shirley Temple doll in all her curls and the dress I made her. Don looked smart, too. In the bedroom Michael presented me with a bouquet of purple hyacinths from the garden. He was cradling the flowers in the palms of his hands, commenting on how much he liked their scent. The stems of the hyacinths were pitifully short. Dora must have

Chapter
37

Easter Sunday

given him permission to cut them without telling him these garden flowers aren't usually picked for bouquets. Of course I didn't mention this fact, either. Instead I told him that I had a present for him, too. I told him my secret. He was overjoyed at the news and at breakfast held my hand under the table.

The church was decorated with some of the same daffodils that had been nodding on its front lawn days before. I loved singing the hymns about Christ our Risen Lord. The quartet was superb. What a blending of voices!

On the drive home Mrs. Emma Cook came in our car and Mr. Pease rode with Bob and Dora. Mrs. Cook seemed to enjoy the passing scenery immensely. She never took her gaze off of it even once as I spoke. For most of the drive she was quiet, her memories entertaining her, most likely. I hope it was that and not the speed at which Michael drove.

After Dora's wonderful dinner the women and children sat in the kitchen and the men retired to the parlor. I enjoyed the company of Mrs. Cook immeasurably. "Call me Emma," she said. I felt uncomfortable at that since for so many years I had called her by her surname. Then to the children she said, "Call me Grandma." In just one afternoon the children were adopted as her grandchildren and she as their grandmother. She has always had a natural rapport with children and seems to thrive on their attention. I feel sad for her that her own grandchildren live so far away.

Emma told us a story about an Easter morning when her girls were small, which gave Emily an idea. Scampering out the door, she returned in a little while with a box containing six baby chicks, which she proceeded to play with on the floor by the woodstove.

"How's Tailgate doing?" Don asked Emily.

"Oh, he wasn't around," she replied brightly.

"Out chasing something, I 'spose," added Don.

"No, he's gone," said Dora.

"Gone?" I asked.

"Yes, we ate'm. He was too mean. He made a nice broth, though."

"Pop goes the weasel," Emma said, and to my surprise, Emily smiled.

Reliable, as dedicated to nosiness as any dog, ambled over to the box of chicks to have a sniff and a taste, too, evidently, because there was a chick dangling on his tongue a moment later. "Down!" commanded

Don sharply. Reliable looked guilty, but couldn't rectify the situation, since the fuzzy feathers stuck the chick fast. It was peeping with all its might. I picked the poor thing off carefully and saved the day. It was actually quite comical. Emma thought so, too.

"Bring the chicks back to the mother hen. They've had enough excitement for one day," I said after a while, noticing that the chicks' heads were bowed and their eyes were tightly closed. Then I walked down the front hall to the parlor, intending to remind Michael that it was time to take Emma home. Hearing the men talking about the history of Appleton and the problems confronting its farmers today, I paused to listen. They were discussing the new government regulation requiring pasteurization. Michael seemed to be taking a strong interest in the conversation, and was subtly giving business advice in the guise of asking questions. What does he know about farming?

We drove Emma Cook home and, as we pulled up to her house, I remembered visiting it as a child. She had a Sunday school party once a year for all the pupils of the church. I recall that she started running her big house as a tourist home after Dr. Cook died. Most of the rooms were closed off in winter, but were always filled by late spring and remained so until early autumn. It was a grand house once. I wonder how she manages now. The house is in disrepair. It needs painting, the picket fence needs mending, and one of the shutters is crooked. Nevertheless, its pair of overgrown forsythia bushes at the entrance of the front walk gave it a cheerful look. Daffodils, dandelions, and forsythia together impart a rhapsody of yellow in springtime.

Tomorrow we leave for home. Michael agreed to sing in the quartet on Memorial Day, so we'll be back for another visit next month.

~

Ladybug — Hippodamia conergens
Forsythias — Forsythia
Hyacinths — Hyacinthus

~

The ladybug and the praying mantis can be purchased through the mail. Some seed catalogs sell them to gardeners because they prey on bugs that nibble on the vegetable garden. Both of these insects happily inhabit suburbs. Have you found either in among the shrubbery?

Spring

Knowledge for Knowledge's Sake

May 1936

As springtime unfolds, my mind is on evaluation. Months ago I wondered how I would go about giving my children grades. I don't give them frequent tests because I know how well they understand what I've read to them or what they read on their own through their ability to narrate. They've showed effort in trying to do their best and, as a result, they have made progress. This satisfies me. Therefore I haven't felt the need to give them grades. I certainly wouldn't want to grade their Nature Notebooks. I think a "Well done!" now and again is enough encouragement, and when their Notebooks are full, the finished project will be its own reward. Then I found something in Charlotte Mason's *Home Education*, where she claims that any system of grading will "distract the attention of children from their proper work, which [should be] in itself interesting enough to

Chapter
38

secure good behavior as well as attention."[1] To get good grades in school is the motivation used in a system of education where children are constantly quizzed and tested. Here at home we are following a *method* of education — we are not participating in a *system*. It's been such a freeing way to teach. I've aimed at learning for the sake of knowledge and not for grades or prizes. Miss Mason recommends that children gain knowledge in three areas: knowledge of God (Bible), knowledge of man (history/humanities), and knowledge of the universe (science/math). Keeping these three areas in mind has helped me in my efforts to be a more orderly sort of person and to cover what is essential to know. I will write Michael's sister and tell her how much of a help her recommended reading has been to me. I do believe she will be glad to hear from us. I should have written sooner.

~

How much learning will your child undertake for knowledge's sake alone?

Watching and Waiting

There are baby robins in the nest. Father robin is keeping them fed — as well as his mate and himself. What a job! If I open the parlor window in the morning we can hear the babies peeping during our breakfast. The sweet sound travels through the house. No change in mother robin and she still hasn't sung a note.

Job hunting has been discouraging, Michael says, because as soon as the interviewer finds out he was let go, interest fades. He has followed up all his contacts to no avail. He has become apologetic and thinks that if he had been placatory during his last weeks with his old company he wouldn't have been let go. Today he admitted sadly, "Integrity is no fence against calamity" — a quote of Mathew Henry's — but he is still hopeful.

Meanwhile I've been making simple meals — oat-

Chapter
39

meal every morning, for instance. I've used up all my canning and root vegetables from the cellar and have taken to baking my own bread again. But I'm not worried. I'm really not. My thoughts have been on Psalm 37:25. King David spoke out of experience when he said, "I have been young, and now am old; yet I have not seen the righteous forsaken, nor his seed begging bread."(KJV) I have a memory of long bread lines and soup lines in the streets downtown but I will not let the scene haunt me. I know David's words are not a promise from God,

but I believe that those who live by godly principles will be blessed. Even if I'm not worried, it doesn't mean I don't long for the day Michael finds work.

The children and I busy ourselves with learning. This is one way I've kept from worrying, and I find it lifts the spirit to be always learning something new. Today Don and Emily were watching ants while I hung up some clothes to dry.[1] They are probably the same ones that are scouting out my kitchen. They watched them dig out their nest, depositing tiny particles of soil, making a mound at the entrance to the nest. They watched one ant drag a sun-dried, shriveled-up piece of earthworm across the driveway. Don followed another ant as it traveled through a maze of grass and off toward our neighbor's property. When I came over to take a peek at these "fantastic ants," I saw that wild strawberries were growing in the grass around the anthill.

"We have strawberries in our yard after all," I reported to Emily. She was expecting to see big red berries, but instead there were only little white flowers. I explained to her that when the flowers are pollinated, part of the flower will become a tiny strawberry. One thing nature has been teaching my children is that in life it is necessary to wait. "All good things come to those who wait," my mother used to say. I'm bearing this in mind about our family's current circumstances, too. I will look for a picture book at the library that describes pollination for her in a little more detail, and perhaps I'll find one on ants as well. The information on ants in my nature *Handbook* is prefaced with this verse:

> *My child, behold the cheerful ant,*
> *How hard she works each day;*
> *She works as hard as adamant*
> *Which is very hard, they say.* —Oliver Herford

The sunflower seeds we planted indoors last week have sprouted two inches tall in their cups. I'll let the children plant them as soon as danger of frost is past. I think it's a good idea to have the children draw the sunflower plants in stages — a sort of growth chart.

~

Little black ant — Monomorium minimum
Strawberries — Fragaria

~

Watching and Waiting

Ants can live in the cracks of the pavement as well as on a bare patch in your lawn. Take ample time to watch them wherever you find them.

～

Can you recognize the wild strawberry?

Tulips

I've been reading to the children about the customs and beliefs of ancient civilizations for most of this school year. At present we are reading about the Middle Ages and I think we will conclude this year's study with this period. I've been happy with our main text, as it focuses on the story and the "people" aspect of history — as recommended by Charlotte Mason.[J] Library books have been very helpful in supplying us with pictures and other details when we want them. Using tracing paper, the children trace pictures from these books to use on a timeline. The only place I could find to hang the timeline was along the wall going up the staircase. I haven't drilled them on names and dates, yet the timeline has been a way to highlight some of the more significant people and events. Michael has been walking to the library with us and has borrowed a book for himself! He

Chapter 40

Spring
~150~

Tulips

has taken to reading history at night; he says he's getting fed up with the newspaper. In the morning at breakfast he tells us what he is learning about the knights of old and life within castle walls. Now I have three narrators in the house.

Speaking of history, I read a little about the history of tulips out of my nature *Handbook* — how they were all the rage in the Netherlands a little over a hundred years ago. Across the street Mrs. Thurston has a few purple tulips growing in the middle of a little bed of purple Johnny jump-ups (wild pansy). What an odd combination, but a pleasing one! I once thought of the Johnny jump-up as a weed. They will take over the garden if they get the chance. In a book on Colonial herbs, however, I read that the seed of the Johnny jump-up was advertised in Boston in 1760, and Jefferson reported planting it in his garden in 1767.[1] At the park the children spotted beautiful red tulips, and outside the library there are some that are a creamy shade of apricot.

⁓

Today Mr. Thurston knocked on our door to announce that he thought it was a good day to let the mother robin free of her splint. His experience with canaries has given him the confidence to handle this wild bird deftly. We all cheered when she flew onto the porch railing. As the day progressed she joined her mate in feeding her little ones.

⁓

The children planted their sunflower seedlings outside.

⁓

**Johnny jump-up (heart's-ease) — Viola tricolor
Tulips — Tulipa**

⁓

Tulips

Pansies are fun to draw because they have flat colorful faces. Tulips are easy to draw by silhouette. Violets have heart-shaped leaves. Which aspects of plants and flowers make them either easy or difficult to draw?

Memorial Day Weekend

Today was a difficult day for me. It started out fine I suppose but as the hours progressed I found myself in a tizzy. Here is how it began. We've had a steady drizzle of rain for five days — very belated April showers — so that when the day came for us to travel again to Bob's, somehow we all expected to set out in sunny weather. Instead, we drove in fog and mist. I wasn't up to the drive — I was still feeling queasy. Michael, though, made the trip a pleasant one with his positive conversation and questions to the children about Uncle Bob's farm. I do believe he is becoming more talkative.

When we arrived, Dora cooked us some tender dandelion greens with chopped green onion and made an omelet with asparagus and a bit of bacon. She popped corn in the leftover bacon grease. It was a tasty lunch. I appreciated the fresh eggs, but only nibbled. During the wash-

Chapter
41

Spring
~153~

ing up I was eager to have some lady's chatter — too eager perhaps, because I don't think I let Dora say much. She did ask me question after question about how my mother did this and that, which got me going. Garrulous, my tongue was on a roll. I'm afraid I might have given her too much advice on rural living. Yet Dora seemed appreciative in her quiet way. When we'd finished washing up, she told me Emma had asked her to send me over for a visit after lunch — about two o'clock. Her countenance was full of expression. Michael seemed curiously keen on the idea when I told him. When I had come downstairs from freshening up I was surprised to hear Dora announce that he and the children were waiting for me in the car.

I opened the car door and said, "It's only half-past one. Won't we be rather early?" He checked his watch and gave me a peculiar reply.

"Yes, well, I'm trying to pay heed to your advice to drive more slowly on country roads."

When we reached the cemetery with Emma's house in view, we were twenty minutes early! With another glance at his watch Michael pulled up to the cemetery. He and the children like reading gravestones. The sky brightened just a bit as it turned from gray to misty white overhead. The air was fresh, cool, and moist. The grass, which was getting noticeably higher, hadn't yet been cut and was covered with creeping phlox blooms — purple, pink, and blue, growing wild about the place. It looked as if heaven had sprinkled the graveyard with them. Thus, Michael and the children learned the name of another flower today.

We wandered. The grass around my mother's and father's gravestones had been hand clipped. I couldn't bear to stay longer than a moment. "Mom, aren't these Grandma's and Grandpa's graves?" asked Don. Wasn't he too young when they died to really remember them? I've been able to put their deaths out of my mind these last four years, but today, standing there looking down at their graves, I was face to face with it. Daddy had suffered such a horrible death by lockjaw and mother had died soon afterwards. One kick in the chest by a lame horse had taken her away from us quite suddenly. I couldn't bear the memory of it, so I turned my face away. Then the children consoled me — unknowingly — with, "Mother, look over here!"

There is a pile of stones surrounding three sides of the cemetery —

Memorial Day Weekend

a wall of sorts. The north side is wooded with a few neglected apple trees, young maples, and some white pine. There, on the outside of the stone wall, were more than a hundred lily-of-the-valley plants growing thickly. Most of them had no blooms, but a good many dangled their white bells. My imagination began to work. Probably years ago a pot of fading lilies (their season for flowering over) was thrown over the wall into the woods — no longer wanted as a grave decoration. The plants must have taken root and over the years multiplied. What other explanation could there be? The children climbed over the rocks and picked some for Emma and some for Dora. Emily thinks they are the sweetest little bells. I agree. Their fragrance is intoxicatingly sweet and their bells are so delicate.

We heard a succession of squeaky chirps coming from several places along the rock wall. Such chirps could have easily been mistaken for the noise of an excited bird.

Michael noticed the noise and said, "What's all the fuss about?"

Unbeknownst to us were chipmunks eyeing us from between the rocks. It was only after we heard the rustling of leaves that our attention was drawn to one chipmunk's new, safer position. When the small striped fur creature knew it was found out, it kept still and silent and so did we. But as soon as we turned to go, their springtime squeaking began again. Calling and answering were heard up and down the row of rocks as loudly as ever.

"What a racket!" said Don.

Michael checked his watch once more and urged us to go on to Emma's so we wouldn't be late. I was glad to leave the cemetery.

Emma's house is less than a hundred yards up the lane. We could have walked but we took the car in case of rain. Why was I so nervous? How I knew something was up I can't explain, but something *was* up. When Michael and I were comfortably seated in her spacious parlor we found out what it was. She explained her proposition, saying that her house is too much for her to maintain alone, as a home for herself or as a tourist home, and that although she has been asked to move to the Midwest to live with one of her daughters, she is distressed at the thought of leaving her home and her hometown of Appleton.

"In short," said Emma, "I am inviting you to make Blackberry Inn your home."

Memorial Day Weekend

Ought I be overjoyed at this, when the offer puts a wrench in my plans? I am looking forward to Michael resuming his career in the city. I like my electricity, being able to walk to the large library, see shows on occasion, window shop, etc. Moving back out here would be a kind of regression.

"The house will be yours when I die if you can put up with living with an old lady until that time," she continued. "There will be work to do on the house, in the garden, and there will be many kitchen chores, especially in spring and summer... beds to change, sheets to wash, those sorts of things." Michael thanked her over and again, and told her we would prayerfully consider her generous offer. I was quiet, echoing his thank-yous and nodding politely. In the car, however, Michael wanted to know if I was feeling ill, because he thought I wasn't my usual self. When we drove past the cemetery, Mr. Pease was mowing the grass for the Memorial Day service and all the phlox were disappearing under the mower blades. Actually I hadn't been feeling any nausea until then.

Back at the farm, I quickly excused myself to run upstairs to my room. I was devastated. I wanted to cry but no tears would come. Must I return to this place of my parent's death? If so, how will I cope? I was in a dark mood, my strength of mind crumbling into pieces, but I somehow hung on to one thought: the Lord is my strength. I prayed. After I had done that, I felt better. God knows my disappointment about Michael's career and I mustn't allow myself to be drenched in self-pity. He doesn't despise sorrow, but He does hate self-pity. I do want to trust Him. He's given me a good husband and I must keep an open mind when we talk the matter over later. For now I ought to pull myself together, join the family, and help with supper. And so I close.

⌒

Eastern chipmunk — Tamias striatus
Lily-of-the-valley — Convallaria majalis
Phlox — Phlox

⌒

Spring

Memorial Day Weekend

Have you ever caught the scent of the lily-of-the-valley?

~

Creeping phlox makes a dazzling ground cover.

~

Have you ever heard the calls that a chipmunk can make? Not only do they squeak but they also do a fast roll of chattering.

The Darling Buds of May[1]

Last night Bob, Dora, and Michael were quiet. There was the same awkward silence at breakfast. This morning after the church service the little congregation was talkative enough among themselves, but toward me they were carefully guarded. I reminded myself that in the country news travels with miraculous rapidity. I felt like I was suspended in one of those long pauses in a chess game — all of Appleton waiting for my next move. It is an understatement to say that I felt self-conscious. In no way could I manage a "winsome countenance" like a heroine in a Jane Austen novel but I was composed. Without Bob speaking a word, I could hear his emphatic statements about the health and morality of country living. He, ever the gentleman, and Dora, his gentle lady, patiently waited. Michael's deportment was impeccable. It hid his anticipation well. His patience was a glaring contrast to my distress.

Chapter
42

The Darling Buds of May

On the way home from church, Michael drove back to the farm the long way. He took the high road that goes along Appleton Ridge, to give the children a view of the shimmering waters of Mirror Lake down in the valley. He sighed and said, "It takes my breath away to see the lake from up here." He said something else, too, but I wasn't paying much attention. The hymn that Mr. Pease had played on his merry organ had clung to me. I was humming the tune, verbalizing only in my head, as I surveyed the passing scenery. I knew the first three verses of the hymn by heart. They were a comfort to my soul as I repeated them:

Fairest Lord Jesus, Ruler of all nature,
O Thou of God and man the Son;
Thee will I cherish, Thee will I honor,
Thou my soul's glory, joy, and crown.

Fair are the meadows, Fairer still the woodlands,
Robed in the blooming garb of spring;
Jesus is fairer, Jesus is purer,
Who makes the woeful heart to sing.

Fair is the sunshine, Fairer still the moonlight,
And fair the twinkling, starry host;
Jesus shines brighter, Jesus shines purer,
Than all the angels heaven can boast.

~

In the early afternoon, Michael and I sat down on an old wooden bench in front of the overgrown lilac bushes. Every trace of morning mist had cleared and the sunshine was warm and bright, somehow filling me with

The Darling Buds of May

hope. The lilac bushes have grown enormously and they are so full of potent purple clusters that they are a wonder. What other plant is so unattended for fifty weeks of the year and yet brings forth a more impressive show of flowers for two of them? Reliable and the children entered our corner of the garden, but Michael skillfully shooed them away. Obeying his tactful suggestions, the lively actors disappeared into the bushes — their energetic exits leaving the heavy fragrance of lilacs fluttering in the air as if being carried on imaginary butterfly wings.

Thus was the stage set for what turned out to be a momentous conversation. I only convey tidbits of it here. Firstly, I was astonished to learn that Michael has had a desire to move to the country since the night we were out under the January stars. At the same time, his interest in his career had been waning. When I heard this, I thought perhaps it was because he was brought up, like Dora, near the city, and might be entertaining romantic notions about country life, notions far removed from reality. I cannot forget how my parents wearied themselves, though they tried to conceal this from their children. He seems, however, quite sober about the idea of moving us out here. Apparently he had been giving it a lot of thought before we received Emma's offer. He mentioned that we could still drive into town, and pointed out that it is less than an hour's drive. If he took a job at home at the corner grocery it wouldn't be enough to pay our rent and car maintenance and we couldn't keep whittling away at our savings. We could no longer afford to live in the nicer part of town. With a big garden in the country we needn't spend so much money on food, as we would be growing much of it ourselves. He bid me imagine living in our own grand house with no mortgage in Appleton close to my brother and such a sweet little church. We could have electricity installed with our savings, he said. He'd like to offer his knowledge of business to the people in Appleton — at the grange hall where the farmers get together, at the general store, etc. Most of all, he would be able to spend more time with the lady he loves, the lady of his dreams, as well as with his children. He needn't miss their childhood because he was married to a demanding career in the city. Then he stopped himself abruptly, as if privately coming to the conclusion that he had said enough. It was an enthusiastic and earnest entreaty and I must admit I was wooed if not wholly convinced.

The Darling Buds of May

I paused and breathed in another breath of lilac-sweetened air. I could have discussed the matter or asked to think about it some more. Instead, I succumbed to his entreaty. "I surrender," I told him. I was surrendering to what seemed to be God's will. At that moment a bluebird, perched on the picket fence, sang a few lovely notes and flew off to an apple tree that was still holding on to the last of its pale pink blossoms. "The bluebird's song is the song of a new beginning," Michael said.

I almost blurted out, "How do you know?" But I caught myself. I spoiled the moment less with an unsuppressed giggle. It was as if springtime in the country had waked him from a kind of husband-hibernation. I was still adjusting to this new demonstrative side of him when a breeze passed through the branches of the apple tree, loosening its petals. The petals landed gently upon us like new-falling snow. Then Michael started singing "In the Shade of the Old Apple Tree" with a touch of vaudeville style. It was all too much. Especially as I remembered that it was under such a tree that he proposed to me. How lovely the moment was. I'll never forget it. But the biting black flies brought me back from dreamland as I slapped the side of my neck and both my ankles became noticeably itchy. "There are no black flies in the city," I told him, as I stood up and held out my hand. As we rose, Don and Emily approached — Don with a sparkle in his eyes.

"Mom, please come. I have something to show you," he requested.

"May I have permission to come, too?" teased his dad.

Don led us to the poultry pen. He pointed to one of the hexagonal-shaped openings of chicken wire. The opening was being used to support a tiny wheel of a web. A tiny spider was in the middle of it. "Last fall I found the biggest web. Here's the smallest web and spider I've ever seen!"

"Yes, but this young spider will grow. It will grow all summer and if it lives it may become as big as the garden spider you found last fall," I told him.

"Swell," he said. Even Emily thought it was cute. Don swatted at the flies that congregated around his ears, trying to hold up his clipboard at the same time so he could finish his drawing. He really was determined.

The Darling Buds of May

~

As soon as Michael and I entered the kitchen Bob and Dora were full of congratulations. It must have been the look on Michael's face because neither of us had spoken a word. "Oh, it will be so good to have you close by!" Dora exclaimed. Bob tried to speak but his eyes became watery. He was so happy. Don and Emily bounded into the kitchen to see us all standing in a huddle. They looked into their uncle's face and asked, "Uncle Bob, are you crying?"

Bob wiped his eyes on his red bandana. He stuffed the bandana back into his pocket, and gave the children a sly smile. Then he reached out to pat the top of each of their heads. "How *can* I be sad when I will have two new farm hands?" he teased. With a "Hooray!" he did a sort of Irish jig, swinging his partners, Dora and me, around the kitchen. The children were perplexed until their dad explained. Then they too put in their hoorays. Perhaps time will give me more gladness of heart on the matter — maybe even as much gladness as they apparently all have.

Later this afternoon Pastor and his older sons stopped by with two fresh trout. They were invited to join our little party, but wouldn't enter the house, claiming they were far too wet from an afternoon of fishing to come indoors. Soon the savory odor of fried fish filled the kitchen, and with corn bread, pickles, and more asparagus covered with a cheese sauce, we had a feast. There was maple custard for dessert, as the offerings of the cows and chickens were in abundance. I did much more than nibble at all of these delicious spring dishes. Living in the country will cause my trim figure to disappear, I expect. But perhaps there are things more important in a woman's life than a perfectly trim figure. My dress was a little too snug for other reasons as well.

~

Apple tree — Malus sylvestris
Black flies — Simulium
Brook trout — Salvelinus fontinalis
Eastern bluebird — Sialia sialis
Lilac — Syringa vulgaris

Spring

~

Do lilacs grow where you live?

~

Where there are flowers there are insects. Which insects fascinate you, and which ones do you call bugs because they get on your nerves? How many different kinds of insects can you find in just one hour during a backyard insect hunt? You might be surprised at the variety.

A Face of Generosity

Today was Memorial Day, and there was a great gathering at the cemetery at 10 A.M.

Pastor Bingham addressed the crowd, the quartet sang, and then we all sang "America the Beautiful." A fiddle was played by a wiry-looking youth in a loose-fitting suit. Beside the fiddler stood quite his opposite: a short round man, a veteran of the Great War. The mouthpiece of his flute disappeared into his bushy white beard and moustache when he played. He played with precision and a deep patriotism. I was touched.

It was another cool morning, and cloudy. I looked around and saw Emma. She was standing nearby. Her eyes, the color of irises in twilight, were set off by her blue dress, and were fixed seriously upon Pastor. I knew then that the divine mix of strength and trust in her character would enable her to accept any answer Michael and I would give

Chapter
43

Spring
~164~

A Face of Generosity

her. I felt ashamed of my selfishness in the face of her generosity. Emma is as durable as marble and as gentle as the May's mist, I thought to myself. I'd like someday to be more like her.

At the close of the ceremony a group of young children began a game of tag (Poke the Elephant) and were running around the gravestones on the far side of the cemetery. A few of the elderly shook their heads but the parents let them play happily. As I watched the group of children from a distance I noticed how easily Don and Emily were welcomed into the play, as if they were two necessary cogs snapped into place.

While this play machine was humming, Michael wasted no time. Together we stepped up to Emma and gave her our answer. Emma met the sincere change in my attitude with joy. We offered to drive her home, but she insisted on walking, so Michael offered her his arm. She took it with a confident graceful femininity that made her age disappear, and the three of us headed toward her house, discussing plans as we walked. We decided we could be moved into Blackberry Inn sometime before the first of July. Until then, Emma decided she'd place a notice on her door: "Closed for repairs — Reopening in July." And what a door she has! It is painted the extravagant color of plum and harmonizes with the deep pink blossoms of the crabapple tree that shades her front walk. How lovely! We have only three weeks to make our arrangements.

~

Crabapple tree — Malus coronaria

~

Have you enjoyed a day outdoors lately?

Wrapping Things Up

June 1936

I will miss this bungalow, our walks to the library, our walks to the park, and taking the trolley downtown. Don and Emily are excited about our move and haven't said a word yet about anything they are going to miss. Young children are better at looking ahead, I suppose.

Bob came by today with an empty truck. He said he had never seen so many lupines along the roadside and brought me three of them. "It must have been all that rain we had," he said, handing me the flowers and a bunch of asparagus. He and Michael filled the truck with some of our more fragile furnishings: lamps, mirrors, etc. and left for Appleton. I suggested that they wrap everything with extra padding. I have experienced the rattle of Bob's questionable vehicle. Michael is staying over in Appleton and will be back by the end of the week after he has done some indoor painting at Emma's. I've been cleaning out closets, sorting

Chapter
44

through papers, giving things away, and packing up books and dishes. The children want to help (they have helped some) but there is really not much I can have them do.

Both Don and Emily have completed their arithmetic books. What a good feeling this is! We have completed our history reading, too. I think their composition books have plenty of writing in them. Emily liked copying Robert Louis Stevenson's poems into her book. Writing, however, has not been one of Don's favorite pastimes. He enjoys oral narrations more, and these are always much longer than his written narrations, but this is fine, for the time being. I like the freeing advice of Charlotte Mason — that children simply and naturally tell about what they've read — or about any experience, for that matter. There is no need to "teach" composition in these early years, she says, if children are given a steady diet of good books.[K] The rigors of writing do have dividends. Now, at the close of the school year, Don reads over all his entries with satisfaction. Yesterday he especially liked reading aloud to me his earlier passages about the animals in E. T. Seton's book. It gave me pleasure, too. Although we are finished with lessons for the school year, I'd like the children to keep up their reading and continue with their Nature Notebooks throughout the summer. Our sunflower plants are making good progress. They are over a foot high already.

Right now the children and I are sitting in the messy parlor listening to the radio as I write. The station had earlier played "Rosamunde" by Schubert and is now playing Pachelbel's "Canon in D" — two of my favorites. Boxes are stacked in the corners of the room, the rug is rolled up, crumpled balls of newspaper lie here and there. The windows are bare of curtains and wide open to let in the air. But there is no breeze. What a sticky humid day! Perspiration does not evaporate. I feel as though all the dust and grime from packing has stuck to me. Therefore I must close now, take a bath, and read to the children. We have begun *Heidi* by Johanna Spyri, and I am enjoying it as much as Emily is. Don thinks it is okay. He is not too fond of Heidi's friend, Peter. I think he is still a bit down because his goldfish died yesterday, and he said that he wished he had thought of drawing it for his Nature Notebook. Now it is too late. Poor Don.

~

Goldfish — Carassius auratus
Wild lupine — Lupinus perennis

~

Miss Rumphius, *by Barbara Cooney, is a lovely story about a woman who plants wild lupine seeds throughout her village and countryside. It is based on a true story.*

~

If your child has a pet, it could be drawn for his Nature Notebook.

Strictly Wildflowers

Today was a beautiful warm sunny June day. At lunchtime Michael returned with a billowing bouquet of wildflowers. "These are all for you," he told me. I was astounded and at the same time reminded of the scene in Jane Austen's *Sense and Sensibility* in which Willoughby presents Marianne with wildflowers. Wildflowers are a first for Michael. Has he overcome his dislike of bees enough to take a stroll along the roadside to collect them all? There were buttercups, purple vetch, oxeye daisies, white yarrow, yellow and orange hawkweed, honeysuckle, and yellow mustard. A spittlebug was hiding in its lump of bubbles along the stem of the hawkweed. I picked off a leaf and rolled it up to poke at the bubbles, revealing to Don and Emily the shiny little bug inside it. Don drew the spittlebug and Emily drew the daisies. Don, with his keen ability to spot small objects,

Strictly Wildflowers

noticed a little white spider camouflaged in the center of one of the daisies — a flower spider. Emily, wearing a straight face, had Don remove that daisy from her little vase of daisies before she began to draw.

When lunch was finished, Michael announced that since tomorrow was my birthday, he was taking us to the seashore, and that we should be ready to leave in the morning. I spent a good part of the afternoon getting things ready, and here I am sitting up late in bed writing. Michael fell asleep with the light on. He must have done an awful lot of painting during his week at Emma's. Earlier this evening I was reading — for my own edification — some of Wordsworth's poems in an old poetry anthology I found at the library. I was searching for anything written about any of the wildflowers that Michael had brought me. I found eight lines from "To the Daisy," similar to his more famous poem, "The Daffodils."

With little here to do or see
Of things that in the great world be,
Sweet daisy! Oft I talk to thee,
For thou art worthy,
Though unassuming commonplace
Of nature, with that homely face
And yet with something of a grace,
Which love makes for thee!

~

Buttercup — Ranunculus acris
Cow vetch — Vicia cracca
Flower spider — Misumena vatia
Honeysuckle — Lonicera japonica
Meadow spittlebug — Philaenus spumarius
Orange hawkweed — Hieracium aurantiacum
Oxeye daisy — Leucanthemum vulgare
Spittlebug — Philaenus spumarius
Yarrow — Achillia millefolium

Spring

Strictly Wildflowers

Yellow mustard — Brassica

~

What are the names of the wildflowers in your area?

~

Do you have access to a large poetry anthology that will supply you with poems about nature?

A Picnic at the Seashore

The homemade cards I found at my place at breakfast I cherish. Don and Emily kept an eye on my expression as I read them. Michael gave me a new book, recently published, on the life of Audubon. I love the illustrations and the color prints of Audubon's drawings. I can't wait to read it. What a luxury!

The picnic basket was fastidiously packed and then we were off. As it was midweek, the traffic was light. We knew we were almost there when we started to smell the salt sea air. We breathed deeply to take it in. Sea air is so fresh and delicious. Our parking spot was two blocks from the beach, yet even with our arms loaded, we were too excited to mind. Michael rented an umbrella and soon we were set up.

The children were absorbed in their surroundings. Words cannot describe my joy as I watched them splashing in the foamy waves, building sand castles with moats

A Picnic at the Seashore

big enough to sit in, digging for sand crabs, finding starfish and hermit crabs. Their faces were full of expressions of delight. My only effective inducement to get them to sit under the umbrella out of the sun for an hour was the open picnic basket. More thirsty than hungry at first, they finished most of the lemonade straight away, but became aware of their appetite with the first bites of their sandwiches. Bread crusts were laughingly tossed to the greedy seagulls, and when the picnic basket was empty of food, it was repacked with the seashells we all helped collect. In the late afternoon I enjoyed watching the sanderlings and plovers scurry back and forth on the wet sand along the ebb and flow of the waves.

While the children were happily occupied, Michael and I talked about our plans and some of the work we had ahead of us at Blackberry Inn. Michael painted a glorious picture of our new life in the country as he imagined it would be. I've never seen his brown eyes so full of anticipation. Then we agreed that because my last three babies had been miscarried, we should keep this baby a secret for as long as we could. Just before the drive home, we walked up to a stand and ordered double-dip ice cream cones. We each had two different flavors. Michael whispered to me that he thought the double dip quite appropriate, as I am eating for two. The day was perfect.

~

Black-bellied plover — Pluvialis squatarola
Herring gull — Larus argentatus
Laughing gull — Larus articilla
Hermit crabs — Pagurus armatus
Northern sea star — Arsterias vulgaris
Sand crab — Emerita
Sanderling — Calidris alba

Summer

Blackberry Inn

no Vacancy

Strawberry Preserves

Goodbye to Bridgeton

The truck arrived at eight o'clock sharp just as I was packing away our breakfast dishes. To stay out of the way of the moving men we all took an early morning walk to the park. We went to say goodbye to Patrick Murphy. We were waiting for him when he showed up for work. He said that he hoped we would come back to see him from time to time. We then walked to the library to return all of our borrowed books. Emily commented that it was strange we weren't taking any books out this visit. I explained that we had plenty of other things to transport to Appleton and we didn't want to lose any library books in the shuffle.

George and Pam gave the children a sincere farewell, and Emily played one last game of hopscotch with Pam. Michael and I exchanged a few words with Mr. and Mrs. Thurston on their front porch. In several hours everything

Chapter
47

Goodbye to Bridgeton

was in the truck; it was packed to the utmost. I was dismayed at the amount of stuff we have, but happy that it all fit. After the moving men had left, I swept and mopped the empty house. Just as I had gotten off my feet and sat down on the porch stoop, the landlord came for the house keys. He told us that he was sorry to see us go.

As we stepped into the car, I scanned the sky in my usual manner. To the west the sky was dark and foreboding, and we were heading straight for it. I looked at Michael. He guessed what I was thinking, and said with solemnity, "I don't believe in omens." It was an eerie drive though it was the middle of the day. The wind couldn't make up its mind which way to blow. The children sat motionless, Don staring blankly out of his window and Emily out of hers. It occurred to me, during the strange quietness of the drive, that a study of clouds was in order and would make a good entry for the Nature Notebooks. Why hadn't I thought of it sooner?

We pulled up to Blackberry Inn to find the truck already there. At that moment it began to pour, and the rain hammering on the car was loud. "What a downpour," I said, almost too softly to be heard over the noise. A mature woman ought not to be so frightened of the weather, as I was at that moment. Then the sound of the rain hitting the car changed.

"It's sleet," reported Michael.

Don was all eyes. "Swell!" he said. We sat very still in the car in front of Emma's house until it was over, which, though it seemed forever, was only a few short minutes. "Small showers last long, but sudden storms are short..."[1]

Inside, Emma was serving the moving men vegetable soup and biscuits. Her wholehearted welcome to us was filled with hugs and cheery remarks. She swiftly escorted us to our places at the table and filled our bowls full of the savory soup. I was ravenous. I spooned up my soup without pausing to contribute to the table conversation and liberally buttered not two but three biscuits. I thought I had never tasted such extraordinarily delicious soup and biscuits and I told Emma so. The men stepped outside to begin unloading, the children at their heels. But in a little while Emily was back in the kitchen. "Didn't you hear us calling?" she asked, adding imploringly, "Please come out back. Please come."

Michael and I followed her to the back garden until we were

Goodbye to Bridgeton

behind the carriage house. Don was there, staring out over the field and old apple orchard. "Isn't it lovely?" exclaimed Emily, pointing to the sky. Though the sky above had lightened up considerably, the distant sky was dark and a beautiful rainbow showed up against its dark background in perfect clarity. Michael commented, "I don't think I've ever seen such a complete one. All the colors are there and it isn't broken anywhere!" Then he looked into my eyes. His were dark and commanding. The simple words he spoke had an unexpected affect on me.

"I said I don't believe in omens, but I do believe in promises. I'm going to do my best to make this work," he reassured me, and gave me his hand to make it a vow.

"Me too," was my tremulous reply.

~

When everything from the truck was in the house, we could barely move about the place. During the unloading we did our best to direct the placement of various boxes according to their labeling, but everything appeared to be in disarray anyway. Therefore Michael and I moved boxes to various parts of the house, trying to establish some sort of order. We were given the largest bedroom upstairs. As it accommodates our parlor chairs, it will also be our own private sitting room. By late afternoon I flopped into one of these chairs, feeling like I couldn't move another muscle. It was then that Emma knocked on the bedroom door. "There are beds already made up for you in the guest rooms. No need to search for your bedding at this hour. Your Bob brought me a present — two spring chickens. I made my specialty — Southern fried chicken. You look exhausted. Why not call it a day? You can tidy up and begin the unpacking in the morning." It was obvious to me that Emma had been preparing well ahead for our arrival. What a blessing!

Michael is tucking the children into bed. I'm glad I remembered to put my diary into my purse so I could write tonight. But I can't stop yawning, so I must call it a day.

~

Goodbye to Bridgeton

When was the last time you saw a rainbow? Use a prism at a sunny window to make a rainbow on the wall.

~

Have you ever lain on your back in the grass to watch the clouds? Your children may welcome the idea of keeping a cloud chart for a few weeks.

Emma Cook's Garden

I sneaked out of bed today. It is early morning and I'm writing in the back garden. I had to get up just after dawn, as a crack in the curtains sent sun rays aimed at my face making me wide awake. Everyone else is asleep, I think. I've just taken a solitary ramble in bare feet. Compelled by the beautiful freshness of the morning, I worshiped with "I come to the garden alone/While the dew is still on the roses." I sang the lyrics quietly and prayerfully. The strong rays of a summer's morning make the layer of dew on the grass sparkle. How cool and refreshing and delicious it feels on the soles of the feet.

Michael is feeling guilty about the whole moving experience. He claims that he allowed me to do too much because the day after we arrived I was beset with abdominal cramps. Because of the cramps he insisted I stay in bed for at least three days. We informed Emma of my pregnancy, but

Chapter
48

we still have not told the children. Emma brought me cups of raspberry leaf tea and little sandwiches on trays. I felt ridiculous. We are here to help her, not the other way 'round. While Michael and the children were unpacking their belongings, they came in and out of the bedroom to ask me where this should be placed and where that should be stored. It was frustrating not to be able to set up things myself, especially since I knew that despite their help, I would be rearranging most of it as soon as I was up and about. Acquiescing as patiently as possible to my enforced bedrest, I spent my time reading my new book on Audubon and helping the children with their writing in their Nature Notebooks. I must admit that the rest was good for me.

The first day of our cloud chart project I was told, "But Mom, there are no clouds in the sky today." Frequent glances out my window confirmed this, which postponed my cloud chart idea a bit. But I had something else with which to amuse them. When I came to the paragraph that described Audubon's complaints over his first attempts to draw birds, I just had to read it aloud:

> *"These are all bad," [Audubon] said later. "Very, very* bad! *... I thought I had drawn a bird because I had put on paper some sort of head and tail with two sticks for legs. And, oh! What bills and claws, to say nothing of a perfectly straight line for a back, with a tail stuck in anyhow. Those tails! You know how rudders sometimes get loose from a boat and will fall this way and that? ... Well, those tails were like unshipped rudders. In real life they would have fallen off of the bird!"*[1]

Don found it funny. I told him, "'You see, you're not the only one who was ever discontented with his drawings." I explained to the children that Audubon had a desire to draw birds in a manner unlike anyone else. He sought to accurately illustrate them in action, posed on branches of trees in their habitats, not as dead stuffed museum specimens. Only with persistence, determination, and countless tries did his skill develop; only after a long time was he successful.

After a moment of thoughtful silence, Don asked, "Mom, do you want me to be a famous artist?"

Emma Cook's Garden

"Not necessarily," I said. "That's up to you. I just thought you'd like to hear a little bit about Audubon." He and Emily looked at the colored pages of Audubon's birds with me and thought they were "capital."

⁓

How good it is to be out in this tranquil garden. "The birds, their carols raise..." A male grosbeak flew up to the garden fence just for a moment — his red bib flashing against his bold black and white markings. Moments later a male goldfinch did the same. Can a bird be more yellow? I look around me and see that the perennials are sprawling and could be divided at the roots. Peppermint and thyme crowd out each other. The fragile pink flowers of the bleeding heart have faded and fallen off yet the foliage is still thriving in the shade of an apple tree. The fern-like leaves so completely surround the stone birdbath that one would almost be fooled that the venerable moss-covered monument didn't exist, if it weren't for the birds that congregate there, make their indulgent splashes in relative safety, and return to their trees and begin singing, rejoicing in their cleanliness.

Emma keeps a large informal flower garden inside a rickety picket fence. Some vegetables are planted in rows outside the garden fence. Many, however, are tucked away in raised beds among the herbs and flowers. I find this style of garden relaxing. It's a bit wild somehow. A seemingly random mixture of herbs, flowers and vegetables appears at first glance to be self-seeded, springing up quite on its own. I know, however, that Emma's casual supervision over her plants is actually a skill that is acquired by considerable experience — a great many hours spent in peaceful contemplation of her garden.

A slate and pebble path leads to the house's rain barrel. Because it is in the corner of the garden, it is handy for the waterbearer. On the far side of the garden is another rain barrel where the rain is also collected from the roof of the carriage house. This malodorous barrel brings an offense to the passerby, as it contains manure tea. Emma calls her fermenting concoction, "Victoria's dressing." The results of this dressing, so diligently applied, are lush flowers and vegetables. The fickleness of New England's weather has been unsuccessful at defeating Emma's efforts. Like my mother did, Emma also must anticipate a surprise frost through the soles of her feet on the moist earth as she walks through her garden on a summer's eve.

An additional, more utilitarian vegetable garden will be necessary next spring to help feed our family as well as our hoped-for constant flow of guests. It is not too late, however, to add some more radish, some winter squash, carrots, and lettuce. There is a small patch of strawberries. It's odd that such an established garden should have such a small patch. It looks like the blooms and runners have been pinched. An idea just struck me... we ought to go strawberry picking today before all the strawberries are gone for the season. It's a perfect day for it. The rearranging of the unpacking I'll do another day. I close. I'm so thankful that I haven't lost the baby.

~

American goldfinch — Carduelis tristis
Bleeding heart — Dicentra spectabilis
Peppermint — Mentha piperata
Rose-breasted grosbeak — Pheucticus ludovicianus
Thyme — Thymus

~

Have you ever seen the pictures of birds drawn by Audubon?

~

A homegrown tomato or strawberry is unparalleled in taste and texture to that of a supermarket version. Consider growing a fruit or vegetable with your children or visiting a "pick-your-own."

Bibliomania

July 1936

All morning we canned strawberry jam. Emily and I learned that Emma had planted those few strawberry plants in her garden as soon as she found out that her little "granddaughter" was coming to live with her. Next year there would be strawberries on them if Emily kept their runners and flowers nipped this year. Yesterday at the strawberry field I showed Emily how to pick a strawberry — by the stem. The novelty of the activity excited her. She had no idea there could be so many strawberries in one place. She is quite the little picker, even in the hot sun. Nimbly she went to work, her straw hat shielding her delicate face from the sun, briskly finishing in fifteen minutes — very certain that she had worked for over an hour!

After all the jars were sealed and the boiling had ceased, Emma took a nap. I wandered. What a grand house

Chapter
49

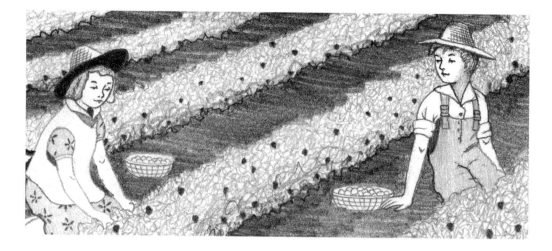

this is! The wide fireplace in the parlor must have seen regular use during the cold winters a generation ago. The parlor itself is an homage to the Colonial period: it is uncluttered and furnished sparsely in the Colonial style. A peek in Emma's bedroom reveals a décor entirely different: it is intoxicatingly Victorian, yet refreshingly bright and cheerful. None of the typical dark maroon velvets shroud her chamber. Instead, the oft-washed fabrics are of faded chintz: a sprinkling of pale red, pink, and orange roses blend into a cream and beige background. The ruffled pillows are bordered with crocheted lace, as is the fireplace mantel scarf. An enormous wardrobe stands beside the fireplace. The drapes are fringed and pulled to the sides with tasseled cords. Family photographs are displayed in ornate frames and painted vases are filled with flowers. Hanging on her wall is a framed verse done in needlework and embroidered with roses, honeysuckle, and morning glories:

> *Gather ye rose-buds while ye may,*
> *Old Time is still a flying;*
> *And this same flower that smiles today*
> *Tomorrow will be dying.* —*Robert Herrick*[1]

Bibliomania

The house has seven rooms downstairs, six rooms upstairs, and four unfurnished rooms in the attic — one of which is a storage room. Two of the smaller rooms will become modern bathrooms. Michael acceded to my wishes, saying that it will be good for business. Emma told us that a retired sea captain built the house. Why he chose not to live closer to the sea is a mystery. Maybe his relatives lived out here. The central stairway is wide and impressive and a circular back stairway off the kitchen winds up to the attic rooms — once the servants' quarters.

Most of the rooms are bright, but the study is darker, as it is lined with bookshelves and is on the north side of the house. This is the room I have been meaning to spend some time in since we arrived, because from floor to ceiling it is full of books. Running a finger along a shelf I ascertained that Emma has been assiduous about dusting them. I tarried here, scanning the shelves, reading the titles on the spines. It is so encouraging (a luxury) to be living in a house with a room full of the books of magnanimous writers. Even though we may not get to the Bridgeton library — nearly an hour away — as often as we'd like, we have an excellent one right here at home. What a blessing! There is a set of history books with woodcuts, Plutarch's *Lives*, and a few biographies. There are novels by Charles Dickens and Sir Walter Scott, the Brontë sisters, Jane Austen, Thomas Hardy, Henry James, and Oliver Goldsmith. (I'd like to read his *Vicar of Wakefield* — I heard that it is funny.) There is a set of Shakespeare's plays and a copy of Lamb's *Tales from Shakespeare* for children, a set of Andrew Lang's fairy tales, and Nathaniel Hawthorne's stories of the Greek myths in his *Tanglewood Tales* and *Wonder Book*. There are novels by Gene Stratton Porter and Louisa May Alcott. I found a tattered copy of *Lorna Doone* by Blackmore, a leather-bound copy of *Gulliver's Travels* by Swift, and two copies of *Robinson Crusoe* — one newer than the other. When I spied Kipling's *Jungle Book* I realized that it would be just the book for Donald. Stevenson's *Kidnapped* and *Treasure Island* would be good ones for him, too. Emily is sure to love *Black Beauty* by Anna Sewell. *A Commentary on the Whole Bible* by Mathew Henry, and two copies of *Pilgrims Progress* will prove insightful. A book of art prints, titled *Famous Paintings — Selected from the World's Great Galleries and Reproduced in Colour*, has an introduction by G. K. Chesterton. It rests

Bibliomania

on its side on the shelf due to its large size. It has one, sometimes two pictures by an artist. I would like to be able to follow Charlotte Mason's recommendation to use at least six of one artist's works to familiarize my children with the signature style of different masters.[L] I am still grateful, however, to have it and would like to start using the book come September. I also found a set of *My Book House*. It is a collection of selected poems, stories, and biographies, profusely illustrated, for children in twelve delightful volumes of graduated difficulty. I thumbed through them and found entries that will be useful for next year's lessons. I was compelled to keep scanning the shelves. There are books on bee keeping, animal husbandry, books on herbs and flowers — books useful for years to come. When I turned to go, I was startled at the sight of Michael in the doorway, leaning against the jamb with his hands in his pockets, staring at me with a boyish grin on his face.

"Oh!" I screeched. "You startled me!"

"Anything look good?" he asked, meaning the books.

"They're marvelous."

"I thought you'd like'm."

"How long have you been standing — or rather, leaning — there?"

"I'll never tell," he teased. He was wearing a relatively new pair of overalls, which were splattered with blotches of white paint. I'm still getting used to seeing him dressed in a tradesman's garment. He looked rather cute, especially with the blot of white paint on the tip of his nose. Neither of us spoke after that. A warm feeling came over me. It was good to have trusted him. When he took my hand in his, to lead me outdoors, I turned his over to have a look. It was his turn to be bearing the signs of living in the country. Palm and fingers were a combination of fresh blisters and new calluses. He's been doing a lot of scraping and painting, indoors and out. Pleased with his work, he wanted me to have a look at the finished bright white façade of Blackberry Inn. It looks splendid! Blackberry Inn will be open for business this coming weekend. He said he wouldn't be able get to scraping and painting the carriage house until next month, though, as there still so much of the outside of the main house to do. What a lot of work he has ahead of him! He was sorry we couldn't be open for business by tomorrow — the 4th of July. It's okay with me as I am in no rush for it.

Bibliomania

~

Books are the backbone of the homeschool. Many a mother enjoys a free hour to scan the shelves of a used bookstore for inexpensive treasures that will be put to good use — books for herself as well as for her children.

~

Some books with a nature theme are listed in the back of this volume.

Fireworks and Fireflies

Just as I had experienced as a child, the modest-sized gazebo was filled with a modest-sized brass band. Families sat on blankets on the village common. Some brought chairs for the elderly. The ice cream that was sold was, as always, strawberry. The drink that was sold was, as always, root beer. Michael was quite the gregarious one. He mingled with the crowd, shaking hands as if he were running for office. I received a welcome from some of Dora's friends. Pastor Bingham's wife Penelope and I had a very nice chat. I rather like her. Her youngest children, Seth and Sara were playing with Don and Emily. Seth had brought his goat and goat cart and he was showing Don and Emily how to manage the reins. While I chatted I watched them out of the corner of my eye, hoping they wouldn't bump into or run over anybody seated on the blankets.

Chapter
50

Fireworks and Fireflies

The evening sky was languid. As is typical with New England's long summer evenings, the horizon was still luminous while the rest of the sky was darkening. Beyond the hills the last lingering rays of sunlight filtered through golden clouds. Each cloud was edged in pink. Soon there would be a short fireworks display. Emma and I, however, were too tired to stay for it. A wave of fatigue came over me that could only be the result of so much strawberry jam-making. Michael thought he'd best drive us home promptly. In the back seat of the car, Don's face wore a droopy pout of disappointment. It was twilight when we pulled up to the carriage house. Michael turned off the engine and paused a moment, looking out past his elbow, which was resting on the open car window. He was the first to notice the fireflies glittering in every nook and corner of the lawn and garden.

Then he called out excitedly, "Come on children, let's catch some lightening bugs! Look at them all! They're everywhere," he jabbered with zeal. Once again my sweetheart had come to the rescue. I don't know where he gets his energy. I went inside with Emma, who meant to retire, but was back outside in an instant carrying some empty jelly jars so that the children could collect the fireflies to use as nightlights. I also knew that in this way these enchanting insects could be exam-

Fireworks and Fireflies

ined more closely. I regarded them as another specimen for the children's Nature Notebooks. In her *Handbook*, Miss Comstock uses this delightful piece of verse as a heading for her firefly chapter:

> And lavishly to left and right,
> The fireflies, like golden seeds,
> Are sown upon the night.

"They're beautiful," Emily breathed happily. "This is fun. They're easy to catch. Look at this one, Mom!"

"Look at all mine, Mom!" said Don, swatting a mosquito that had landed on his outstretched arm.

"I need a jelly jar, too," said Michael. I went inside to retrieve one for him. As soon as I reappeared, the first rocket was heard: "Boom!" A small bit of the fireworks display could be seen over the tops of the trees. "Up to the attic window, you two. Run! You'll see the fireworks more _clearly from up there," I told them. I had not seen Don so excited. He and Emily handed us their jars and ran off. Michael and I made it up the second flight of circular stairs more slowly, but soon all four of our heads were peering out the low attic window. Together we gave out our "oohs" and "ahhs" with the rise and fall of the glittering display.

When we returned to our bedroom — after getting the children off to sleep with their blinking lanterns — there were two glasses of fresh strawberry parfait on a tray. A note beside it read, "I am so glad you are here. Thank you for a lovely day, With fondness, Emma." It was then that I realized that we had been so involved in our amusements that none of us had given Emma as much as a "Goodnight." Michael was already settled into his armchair with a book, smoking his pipe as he is (still) at this moment, and when I mentioned our lack of manners to him, he said, "I'm sure she took neva no mind to it." Country colloquialism did sound strange coming from him. But he proved to me that he was in a teasing mood. He smiled a wide smile, then pulled out his pipe again and added, "It's probably poisoned parfait and if we read the back of the note we'll find that we will die in fifteen minutes unless we pay her a large sum of money for the antidote."

"What book is that you are reading — *The Adventures of Sherlock Holmes?*" I asked.

"How'd you guess?"

⌒

Firefly — Photuris pennsylvanicus

⌒

A bug jar can be used and reused all summer.
Today's child can use a jar of unbreakable plastic.
Have you ever given bed and breakfast to a bug?

Weeding

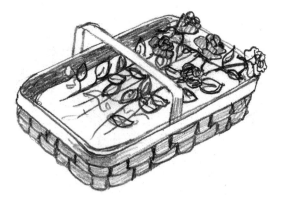

Blackberry Inn opened yesterday, although the bathrooms are not ready — and neither is the installation of the electricity complete. Today we had our first guests. It was agreed that Emma will make breakfast each morning. I'm to make supper during the week. On the weekends when we are apt to have more guests, Emma will make both the breakfast and supper, and the children and I will do the washing up. Emma, at ease with the social graces, takes pleasure in her guests. She lets none of her aches and pains influence her sunny disposition. I know she has aches and pains, because on some mornings she uses a cane and does everything markedly more slowly. This morning after breakfast I caught her in the garden — on her knees — weeding the tomatoes. When I came over to help I asked her how she was feeling. She looked up at me, brushing wisps of unruly hair away from

Weeding

her forehead with the back of a hand. As if to prevent me from saying what I was thinking — something like, "Should you be doing this sort of thing at your age?" — she smiled and said, "My dear, much of the work in this world is done by people who don't feel so very well." Then she more light-heartedly asked me how I was feeling.

"I'm very well, thank you," I told her.

"Will you go for a walk with me, then?" she asked. She bent over the rain barrel, dipped in her hands, and dried them on the towel that hung close by. Then we walked over to the cemetery, just the two of us. Michael had taken the children into the city for the day to do errands. It was the first time Emma and I had been alone together. Emma carried some roses in a shallow basket. She had cut them earlier from the ancient rose bush that climbs the arching trellis next to the carriage house. As we approached the cemetery, I spotted the place where the lily-of-the-valley grow — now without flowers but still thick with leaves. "This is your property all the way up to the cemetery, isn't it?" I asked.

"Yes it is, and the fields behind it, too."

"Then how about if I separate some of those lilies and make a place for them in the front garden next to the lamb's ears?"

"You've noticed the lilies, have you? Yes, splendid. What a good idea! It is interesting to see what the woods bring back to life, isn't it?" She walked circumspectly through the cemetery, lingering here and there between the rows of gravestones, placing her roses on various graves — me by her side. Then she stopped at my parents' graves. The last two roses were apparently for them. She held onto the basket of roses as she spoke. "You don't mention your parents much, dear." Emma was doing further weeding. This time it was the weeds of my heart.

"That doesn't mean I don't think of them often. There is so much about life that reminds me of them. But there are some things I cannot think about."

"Oh, you mean their deaths?"

"Yes."

"Horrible, I know, and a shock. You needn't think about it. Aren't there many other memories of your mother and father to occupy you — pleasant ones?"

I stared out at the landscape beyond the cemetery, not focusing my

Weeding

eyes on anything in particular. Bemused and set off guard, I said, "I didn't get to say goodbye to Mother. You know how suddenly she died."

"Yes, and baby Emily, I heard, was too sick for you to leave her and be here for your mother's funeral." Emma's manner was straightforward and kind. Her understanding tone summoned up feelings I had been suppressing for years. I would have listened to anything she had had to say because I respected her experience. I felt safe. She had gone through greater loss than I.

"Perhaps, dear, there are some other things you didn't get to say to her. Perhaps you've carried around guilt because you longed for a different sort of life than she had — a life with less labor — a life with more to see and do — a more modern life in the city?"

"At first I liked being a secretary in a growing company. I liked my paycheck and being able to buy things. That's where I met Michael."

"But the glitter of it subsided when you realized that what you really longed for was a home and children of your own?"

"Yes, that's right. I never admitted this to my mother or honored her by telling her how thankful I was for her love and care, for teaching me by example, for pointing out without words what is the most precious thing in a woman's life — her family."

"I know that because of the distance between her home in the country and yours in the city she couldn't see you as often as she would've liked, but believe me Carol, she understood that rejecting the country life didn't mean you were rejecting her. She used to speak to me with the pleased tone of any grandmother, about how successful Michael was in the company, and how much you loved little Don and baby Emily and enjoyed taking care of them. She was at peace about how she raised you — at peace that you had the Lord. Miss your parents Carol, yes, but be reconciled in your heart before God. Don't hang on to regret. Then, when you see your mother and father by and by, the Lord will have taken care of all that." Her words prompted me to think of a chorus of comfort: "In the sweet by and by we will meet on that beautiful shore..."

Emma held out the basket. Mindful of the thorns, I laid a rose gently on each of my parents' graves. This time I didn't turn my face away. I felt better about things — much better, thanks to the holy emissary in white hair. After one of her understanding hugs, she said, "Flowers placed

Weeding

at gravestones are *not* for the benefit of those beyond the grave. They are for those left behind."

Such weeding could not hinder the growth of our mutual esteem.

~

Later today the electricians finally turned up. I would've liked to go with Michael and the children to Bridgeton but I wanted to hasten the settling-in process and be around when the electricians did whatever it is they do. I went from room to room, perspiring first with the carpet sweeper, then with my flannel-duster, in order to watch their progress unobtrusively. They'll be back again tomorrow.

I was in the kitchen when my crew arrived.

"Mom, we drove past our old place and saw the sunflower plants. They're huge!" Don said.

"That's wonderful," I said. "Any flowers yet?"

"No, not yet."

When the children went out the kitchen door, I thought about how their sunflower growth charts had been interrupted by the move. It's disappointing. Dora probably has a few sunflowers. Maybe the children can continue their charts by drawing hers.

I told Michael about my morning, about what had been troubling me about my parents. I explained what I had kept stashed away until Emma summoned it up gently and bravely. She probably had been meaning to talk to me about it for some time. Anyway, a burden was lifted. Michael was pleased. And I can't be more pleased that my automatic washer will soon be able to be plugged in and that we will soon have faucets with both H and C that work.

~

Roses — Rosa
Tomato — Lycopersicum
Woolly lamb's ears — Stachys byzantina

Summer
~197~

Out in the Fields with God

Michael has made a large sign for the front lawn. He painted "Blackberry Inn" in neat white letters over a background of the same extravagant deep plum color used for Emma's front door. Don was helping him dig the holes in the ground for it when guests pulled up to the carriage house. Michael stopped his work to greet them, then checked them in, showed them their room, and carried up their bags. On his way back outside, he popped his head in the kitchen to see if I had finished cooking.

"No, not yet," I called after him. "Pretty soon, though." I had a birthday cake in the oven for Emily, was preparing part of the evening meal ahead, and was waiting for the bread to cool so that I could slice it for sandwiches for the birthday picnic. Emma and Emily were at the table shelling peas. Out of the corner of my eye I watched stray

Out in the Fields with God

peas pop out of Emily's pods and onto the floor. Neither Emma nor I mentioned this because we didn't want to discourage our little worker. Instead, Emma gave her a wider bowl. The smaller bowl "full of peas" was taken away with a "Good, good, good; we're getting a lot of peas for our supper, aren't we?" I swept up the runaway peas before they were smashed underfoot. With the temperature of the kitchen rising and so much going on at once I felt myself winding up into a tizzy and could have easily lost my patience if it hadn't been for the presence of such a steadily uplifting grandmother.

"Mmm, the birthday-girl's cake smells delicious," Emma said, spontaneously leaning closer to Emily until their smiling cheeks touched for a moment.

Here at Blackberry Inn guests are served only breakfast and supper, and only during specified hours. Therefore I was able to escape at lunchtime to the brook with my family — and Seth and Sara, who had been invited to join us for the afternoon party. Michael has been teaching Don and Emily how to become better swimmers. He takes the children to the brook whenever he can.

It has been years since I last visited the swimming hole. Once we passed the village and drove just a little further along Appleton Ridge Road, we were met with a panoramic view of the snug valley — its white farm houses, white church steeple, red barns, meadows dotted with cows, blueberry fields, the brook, and the shimmering blue Mirror Lake. I remember now that this was the scene that Michael found breathtaking that day in spring. Today it seemed so much more splendid to me. I had forgotten how green and picturesque Appleton is this time of year. Haymaking was going on all over the valley. We drove downhill on a rather bumpy dirt road until we came to a flat grassy knoll. We parked on the grass beside the covered bridge.

Once everyone was in the water, Michael was master of ceremonies. He repeatedly announced to me the "amazing aquatic skills" performed by the children. "Hey, there you go, Emily! Well done, Don. Seth and Sara, you're doing well, too. Hey, look at that! Did you see that, Carol?"

"Yes, yes, yes," I replied, nodding enthusiastically. I was truly impressed. As I watched Michael play with the children, I saw the joy that has taken root in his heart this summer. Today I sensed joy take root in mine as well. One is often afraid to indulge in happiness because it is so fleeting. But joy is something that has roots. It isn't something that is blown about by the winds of circumstance, so perhaps this joy will always be in reach if we aren't afraid to rest in God's blessings and trust Him wholeheartedly no matter what the circumstances. Don whispered something to the others and the next moment all four children were wildly splashing Michael, laughing with abandon. Michael sank below the water's surface and disappeared, pretending to have drowned. When he didn't rise straightaway, the children poked around for him. Emily's face looked half amused, half frightened. "Here I am," he called at last from the direction of the covered bridge. Having swum underwater, he was hiding in its shadows watching their bewildered faces. "You'd better get out of the shade before you get leeches," I called to him.

The water was cold but I have learned at last the trick to getting in all the way. The trick is to agree with those who are trying to coax you in that it indeed isn't all that cold. It was delightfully refreshing once the initial chill wore off. I can't remember when I've swum last. Emily and Sarah were my swimming companions for a while.

I was successful at protecting our sandwiches and the birthday cake

(from a bumpy ride, ants, and the heat of the sun) just long enough for them to be eaten. The children, eating quietly on a blanket in the shade, noticed the dragonflies. They all glistened in the sun, but one iridescent blue one stood out from all the rest. They spotted a red-winged blackbird on a dangling branch of a weeping willow, almost hidden by the tall grass. In a stagnant shady pool of the slow-moving brook, some water bugs twitched and magically glided over the water. Below the surface of the bronze-colored water were tadpoles and minnows. Don asked if he could use the empty lemonade jar to bring one home. I told him it was a good idea since he had never gotten to draw his goldfish. Although they were absorbed in the company of their playmates, the children noticed all this nature without me pointing any of it out to them. I hope to return with our clipboards another day.

There is a poem attributed to Elizabeth Barrett Browning that expresses my new-found joy:

～

The little cares that fretted me,
  I lost them yesterday,
Among the fields, above the sea,
  Among the winds at play;
Among the lowing of the herds,
  The rustling of the trees,
Among the singing of the birds,
  The humming of the bees.
The foolish fears of what may happen,
  I cast them all away
Among the clover-scented grass,
  Among the new-mown hay.
Among the rustling of the corn,
  Where drowsy poppies nod,
Where ill thoughts die and good are born —
  Out in the fields with God!

～

Out in the Fields with God

It was a lovely afternoon, that is, until we returned home. As soon as Emily stepped out of the car — barefooted — she drew back with a sharp exclamation, eyes large with alarm. A bee had stung the side of her foot. She was noticeably upset. Emma appeared seemingly from nowhere: no one saw where she had come from. No doubt she was in the garden and saw at once what had happened. "Do you have a dollar?" she asked Michael.

"Yes, I do," he said, stepping forward solicitously.

Emma folded up the dollar he gave her and flicked off the stinger with it. Then she reached over and picked a weed from the grass. She told me to put two of the leaves in my mouth and chew them up. I obeyed, after a moment's hesitation, while my family looked on in silence. "Good," she said. "Now hold the poultice you have made on Emily's sore foot."[1]

"Grandma, what weed is it?" asked Don.

"It's the plantain. The Indians called it 'white man's footsteps' because its leaves lie flat in the grass, and wherever the white man settled, these plants sprang up.[2] The seeds were carried over in the ships, probably mixed with hay or wheat. When the forests were cut and crops were planted, these plants spread. Here, look, can you see the fiddle strings?" Emma folded back the stem of a plantain leaf and scraped part of the stem away with a fingernail. Voila! Four fiddle strings!

Don, looking over Emily's shoulder, said, "Now all we need is a bow."

I was proud of Emily. She shed not a tear. "Thank you, Grandma," Emily said with genuine appreciation. The poultice, the story, and the violin strings in her hand had a calming affect on her. I would have preferred to be given some credit, too, for my willingness to be used as an emergency mortar and pestle. But alas, good deeds should sometimes go unnoticed. It keeps one humble. Later I asked Emma if she would pass along her knowledge of herbs to me. She said, "Of course, dear."

~

Common waterbug — Cerris remigis
Dragonfly ("Northern bluet") — Enallagma cyathigerum
Fathead minnow — Pimephales promelas
Freshwater leech — Macrobdella decora

Out in the Fields with God

Green frog — Rana clamitans
Plantain — Plantago rugelii
Red-winged blackbird — Agelaius phoeniceus

~

Is there a brook or other body of water nearby?
What kinds of wild life live there?

Crickets

I am beginning to feel settled into Blackberry Inn and also into a summer evening routine. Guests eat with our family in the dining room. I have the children change out of their play clothes and into something more formal for the evening meal. Michael and I change, too. Dressing for the evening meal is a tradition of Emma's. She loves cooking for people and once her apron is off — just before she sits at the table — it is off for the rest of the evening, as the children and I do the washing up. Emily likes to set the long table and pick flowers for it. It's good for the children to be present at the dinner table, as they are able to hear some interesting adult conversation, hear about travels, or business, or opinions on music, art, and sometimes politics. They are excused early — sometimes very early, if Michael detects any opinions of the clientele that he doesn't much care for.

Chapter

53

Crickets

The dining room is one of my favorite rooms of the house. It is a soothing, elegant room — a room that looks as if that eminent designer, William Morris, had had much influence. As the descending sun creeps 'round to the west side of the house, it lights up the golden horn of plenty — a stained glass window above the buffet. The fireplace on the opposite wall of the room will provide more glowing light on long winter evenings. A cherry mantle frames the fireplace. A built-in china cabinet and pocket doors separate the dining room from the entrance hall. The pattern of Emma's dining room wallpaper is pale green vines with heart-shaped leaves that climb up to the ceiling, with soft blue morning glories scattered along the vines.

After the meal Michael usually clears the table. Sometimes he keeps us company in the kitchen. This is where we decided to keep our radio so we can listen to music or a show while Emily and I do the dishes. (Don has gotten used to hearing his show with a broom in his hand.) At other times Michael sits in the parlor with the guests. He quietly puffs on his pipe, reverting back to his reticent self, but occasionally he makes a remark or two to show deference to the speaker. After removing my apron I often sit in the parlor for a few moments before the children and I go upstairs to read *Heidi*. Most evenings Michael enters the children's room to read them a paragraph of Scripture. He will also, at times, to close the evening, carry his Bible downstairs and read aloud a paragraph to any guests we may have. With a "Goodnight," he turns out the parlor lights. At this, the guests understand that it is time for all to retire upstairs. Emma is comforted by this custom. She likes having a man in the house again and has told him that. She also shared with me that Michael's careful diction (in baritone resonance) and subtle inflections reveal the high regard in which he holds the Scriptures.[M]

Today was a calm day. The evening consisted of our typical summer routine except for a small interruption. I believe it is the curiosity of children that keeps life from drifting into mere routine. In the morning Don wanted to know why there are fewer songs sung by the birds now when he awakes — what a keen observation! I admitted that the woods are a lot quieter now in late July than they were in May and June. Also the thick summer foliage makes the birds nearly invisible. Nature seems to make up for this with the crickets that chirp in rhythmic syncopation all evening.

Crickets

"It's the crickets' turn to make music," I told him. During the day he had collected some in a bottle. Tonight we were all startled during my reading of *Heidi* by the sharp high notes of a cricket coming from under Emily's bed. One glance at Don's bottle and I saw that the top was off.

"How many crickets did you have in that bottle?" I asked Don. He shrugged his shoulders. He couldn't remember. The three of us set about looking for them — the children dusting the floor with the knees of their pajamas. Before long the house was too dark and we discontinued our search. I placed the bottle, with lid secure, outside the kitchen door and then went back upstairs to finish my reading.

Something else sets this day apart for me. When I closed our storybook, Emily made a confession. She told me that she would feel just as sad as Heidi if she had to live in a city and see mostly buildings, very little sky, no green fields, no ponds, no hills. "Are we going to stay here?" she asked. "I hope we never leave," she added as I tucked her in. I didn't make her any promises but I did say I liked it here, too. Grown-ups often give children little lies to keep them happy. They believe it their duty to keep them happy this way. But I wasn't lying to her. I honestly do like it here.

A moment ago I put down my pen. But I have picked it up again to add one more report. There was a succession of high-pitched chirps coming from one of the guestrooms, followed by a grunt, heavy footsteps, the sound of a piece of furniture moving across the floor, and then a distinct thud. Michael, roused from his reading, asked, "What was all that?" I knew exactly what it was and explained. But I won't say a word of it to Don tomorrow.

~

Field cricket — Gryllus pennsylvanicus

~

Listen to the sounds of nature both at daylight and at night.

~

Crickets

It was an entomologist who discovered that the common black cricket's notes are pitched at E natural, two octaves above middle C. Only the male cricket scrapes its wings together to make its characteristic chirp. The female, it seems, has more practical matters to attend to.

The "H" Is Working

All the indoor plumbing is now complete. We actually have not one, but two bathrooms, each with its own bathtub! Emma is delighted, because the first floor bathroom is adjacent to her bedroom. Both have hot water. I wish I had a bottle of champagne to celebrate!

The installation of the electricity has also been completed, which means my Maytag has been very busy. I've had dirty laundry stored up for this momentous occasion. My laundry was spread in sorted piles about the kitchen floor this morning, as I don't have enough baskets to contain it all. Michael came into the kitchen for a cold soda pop. He had been raking and pulling weeds from the gravel.

"You two sound like school girls," he commented, as he watched me demonstrate my machine. Emma and I hung rows of white sheets across the backyard clotheslines.

Chapter
54

The "H" Is Working

The sun and breeze were very cooperative this wash day: rows of bright sheets, tea towels and under-things waved in the warm breeze. Such a spectacle seemed to have caught the notice of a curious crow that flew into the yard for a closer look. He first paced the premises like a Scotland Yard inspector. He perched himself on the garden fence, then on the trellis, then on the edge of a clothesline. I watched Don and Emily in the distance clamber out of the twisted branches of an apple tree and run all the way down the grassy hill as soon as they spotted the visitor.

"Mom, there's a funny black bird in the yard," reported Don, my little scout.

"Meet Zorro the Crow," Emma matter-of-factly stated. "He comes around when there is a lot of washing out." She failed to tell us why. We returned to the house to run the next batch of washing through the ringer. Don and Emily scurried back up the hill to their tree. From what I could tell they were acting out an episode from *Swiss Family Robinson*. When I came outside again with another basket of clean wet washing, I stopped in my tracks, speechless. Several of our clean sheets lay on the ground. Behind our backs Zorro had begun mischievously pulling clothes pins off the line. And he was caught in the act! When discovered, he gave out a loud "Ca-a-aw," then a low broken "Caw," which sounded more like an old hag's cackle. I turned to storm back to the kitchen to complain to Emma, but was prevented, because at that moment Emma was standing calmly on the doorstep, also a witness to this smug bird's crime. She was ready for him. "Give him this," she insisted, holding something small in an outstretched arm and open palm.

"A bottle cap?"

"Yes, he collects them. I never throw him food because I'm afraid he'll come 'round too often, but he seems to be satisfied with anything shiny... for a while, anyway."

Agitated, I protested. "This black bird is a blackmailer."

"He doesn't realize he is spoiling the washing, he just knows what will get my attention."

"Mom, Mom, the crow is on the clothesline and..." reported Don, out-of-breath and a little late — not too late though for him to be the one to give the bottle cap a good throw far out into the yard, away from the clotheslines. Zorro dove for it and gracefully flew away, contented.

Summer

The wash hung on the lines undisturbed the rest of the afternoon. While it dried I had lunch with the children. Our picnic blanket was spread in the orchard under their favorite apple tree. After we ate I rested on the blanket and read to them out of my nature *Handbook*. I read portions from the cricket chapter, and the chapters on dragonflies, on frogs, and on crows. I was on a roll and, making up for lost time, I asked the children a few questions from the lesson sections.

There was a lot of white clover in the grass. I picked the flowers with their stems and showed the children how to tie them together to make a clover chain. Emily was concerned about the bees buzzing all around the clover flowers, but they moved away when we moved our hands slowly over the clover before we picked the flowers. We kept our eyes open for Zorro, but he never returned.

Summer

The "H" Is Working

The house is full of guests this evening. It is the first time Michael has had to hang out the No Vacancy sign. After supper I was looking forward to a warm soapy bath in my new bathtub. I sneaked the children upstairs to take their baths while the guests were still finishing dessert. Then I came downstairs to do the washing-up in the kitchen. As soon as that chore was finished, I bypassed the society of the parlor and headed straight for the upstairs bathroom. It was occupied. Since then both bathrooms have been occupied this entire evening. I got so tired of waiting that I gave up, got dressed for bed, and sat down to write in this diary. Most of my day has been spent washing. All I wanted was a bit of hot soapy water for myself.

"Carol, it sounds like the bathroom is free," my sympathetic husband said a little while ago.

"Oh," I replied, and left the room briskly. In the bathroom I turned on the tap. Out of the H came cold. Michael was right. The bathrooms are good for business. But what about the lady of the house? I'm not too discouraged, however, because after all I'll no longer be needed to empty the chamber pots.

~

American crow — Corvus brachyrhynchos
Red clover — Trifolium pratense
White clover — Trifolium repens

~

Crows can often be seen in parking lots, strangely enough. Where have you seen or heard one?

~

Have you ever made a clover chain or clover crown?

Farm
Hands

August 1936

It's nighttime. The house is quiet. I have put my knitting down to write. Michael and I are in our easy chairs in the bedroom. I started a pair of argyle socks for him for his birthday and since he hasn't asked what I am making, I've been able to carry on quite out in the open while he reads. I was hoping to be further along in my sock making by now. Even so I had to dig out my diary again — it's been weeks. Writing in bed is something that Michael doesn't mind but I will no longer knit in bed, especially with my size two double-pointed needles. I did this last night and this morning he cleverly confided in me about last night's "so called" bad dream. In it he was a giant Cyclops in a brown suit.

During these bright sunny days of early August, the children and I have been visiting Bob and Dora to help hoe and water their large vegetable garden. Today Michael exam-

Farm Hands

ined Bob's poultry pen with the idea of making a smaller one for Blackberry Inn. With the platters of eggs Emma serves every morning and the number of cakes and muffins we bake, he thinks we should have our own hens. Bob has been very generous in supplying us with eggs and milk regularly, but we are running out of things to barter. He won't take money, so we do all we can to respond to his generosity. Michael has been helping him get the hay in the barn. The dry weather we've had has been perfect for haymaking. I said I'd be glad to take care of Jonathan at the Inn on the days Dora wanted to go into town with Bob, but they declined the offer, sensing how busy I am here. Recently Bob told the children that for every day that they hoe, he'd give each of them a one-year-old layer. Emily is especially happy with this reward for her labor. The children only work an hour or so a day, but between them have earned ten hens that they have agreed to help take care of.

In one corner of Dora's herb garden thrives my mother's yellow garden patch — the one I daydreamed about months ago. It has been well maintained by Dora and is in its full glory with sunflowers and black-eyed Susans. Beyond the garden fence at the edge of the pasture is more yellow — in the form of flowering weeds: St. John's wort, spears of mullein and butter-and-eggs. In between the stones of the garden path grows chamomile. I gathered a handful of the tiny daisy-like flowers so I could later make chamomile tea for the children. What a lovely apple scent the flowers have. I knew Emily would like to sample the same tea that Miss Potter's Peter Rabbit had to take for his tummy ache.

The children were able to draw the final sunflower picture for their growth chart.

"This will be the biggest flower in my book," stated Emily.

In several weeks I hope to return so that the children can see the black sunflower seeds forming on their heavy bowing heads.

Dora had allowed some kitchen herbs to bloom, instead of pinching them back. Hovering over the thyme were bumblebees feeding on the thyme's miniscule purple flowers. Don liked watching them in action, buzzing from flower to flower. Small orange butterflies — the orange speckled with black dots — were also plentiful. The butterflies were hardly noticeable when their wings were folded because the undersides of their wings are simply brownish gray. I identified them with my field guide to be the American copper. I found that I could handle the butterfly with minimal scale loss by very gently grasping it by the wings just above the body and as close to its shoulders as possible. Emily took hold of a butterfly that was preoccupied with feeding. She held it gingerly but it still struggled. I showed her how the butterfly could be calmed when held upside down.[1]

~

One afternoon this week, on the way back from the farm, Michael stopped the car. "What's that in the middle of the road?" he questioned. It looked like a rock.

Don leaned forward, straining his neck to see, and exclaimed, "It's a tortoise trying to cross the road. It's a tortoise!"

"I'd better move it out of the way," Michael said.

"Wait, Dad! May I take it home?"

"What do you think, Carol?"

"All right, but it will have to be returned after a time," I said.

"Swell."

"Yeah, swell," echoed Michael with genuine interest. After he handed the tortoise to Don, my dignified husband did something I had never seen him do before: he spit on his "tortoise-y" hands. Then he wiped them on his overalls!

We stopped the car again at the general store for flour, sugar and bacon. There was a sign that read "Help Wanted — Blueberry Rakers." Michael took down the address and time. I said nothing. When his eyes met my questioning ones, he only smiled and wiggled his eyebrows.

~

The following day Michael did some research. Not confident with his ability to build his own hen house, Michael checked the shelves of Emma's library and found a plan that would be suitable. Emma was happy to hear the news. She had been wanting to have hens again but hadn't mentioned this to us as it's been obvious we've had so much else to do. She showed us the spot where she had once kept her biddies. Then

Farm Hands

she handed Don and Emily each a pail and walked them out to the brambles to pick blackberries. I was in the garden harvesting some ripe tomatoes when they returned with pails full.

"Oh my, what a lot of blackberries," I said, "Well done, children." Later I told Michael that the color of the children's play-clothes now matched the color of his sign out front. He responded with a grin, "We aren't called Blackberry Inn for nothing," adding that he thought they each ought to have a pair of overalls. My little girl in overalls? How dreadful!

After only several days of picking, the kitchen was overrun with blackberries. We had enough to make dozens of jars of blackberry jam. We only stopped our industrious boiling and bottling when Michael returned from the general store with news that it was out of jelly jars. "We aren't called Blackberry Inn for nothing," Emma said, as she screwed the lid onto the last jar. When all the jars were stowed on shelves in the cellar, she disappeared into her room for a nap and I began supper for the family and the guests. I think I ought to make some calico covers for the lids — lavender calico would do nicely. Then I could put a few jars on display and sell them to tourists.

This evening I took a long luxurious bath while Michael read to the children. The hot soapy water revived me but it didn't completely remove all the purple stains from my fingers. "We aren't called Blackberry Inn for nothing," popped into my mind on its own accord as I comfortably rested under the bubbles, enjoying the solitude of my bath.

I will put my diary down and get back to my knitting. Perhaps I can get several more rows done before I get too sleepy.

~

American copper — Lycaena phlaeas
Black-eyed Susan — Rudeckia hirta
Butter-and-eggs — Linaria vulgaris
Chamomile — Chamaemelum nobile
Common mullein — Verbascum thaspsus
Common St. John's wort — Hypernicum perforatum
Thyme — Thymus

Farm Hands

How can you tell the difference between a moth and a butterfly? Leave the back porch light on at night and in the morning identify the moths that rest near the light.

Flavorful either hot or iced, herb tea requires little to no sugar and is much better for you than soda pop. Which herbs can you identify by scent? How about flavoring your food with a new herb this week?

Blueberries

This morning Michael told me he was headed out to the blueberry fields on the ridge. He was wearing his painter's overalls. He tipped his funny cap and was off. By midday he was back. He entered the kitchen with an appetite and a sore, stiff back. We took a walk after we ate because he needed to loosen up and talk to me. I affably accommodated his steps and slowed to a shuffle.

He confided in me. "I wanted to make some extra money so we could hire someone to come and do the washing for the next few months — at least until we close in late October. I'm afraid you're doing too much, Carol. But I just don't think I can continue the raking. It's *very* frustrating." His back really must have pained him because we lumbered along.

I knew very well how the raking of lowbush blue-

Chapter
56

Blueberries

berries doubles the body over. A rectangular scoop with teeth is held by its short handle. The blueberries are raked up with a swing of the arm close to the ground. The scoop is emptied into bushel baskets. It takes a lot of raking to fill one bushel. Blueberry raking is something one must get used to gradually.

"Thank you, Michael, but with my automatic washer I'll do fine. Just don't throw away any bottle caps."

"Oh, yeah," he snickered, but snickering hurt. "Oooww," he moaned.

"Please come inside and lie down."

"I guess I should. I'll work on the hen house later."

It was thoughtful of Michael to wish me to have less work to do. It would be wonderful to have more help 'round here.

~

There was a steady drizzle of rain all afternoon. Regardless of this Don kept popping outside to "check" on his tortoise. I assured him of the creature's well being.

"Mom, the field guide says this is a boxing turtle," he said.

"Yes, it is."

"Are turtles and tortoises the same thing?"

"Not exactly. Because the boxing turtle spends its time exclusively on land, it should properly be called a tortoise. Turtles spend much of their time in or around water and have legs and feet more for swimming."

"Oh," he said, and shrugged his shoulders. He showed me the life-size picture he had drawn of it. The problem was that it was too big to fit onto the pages of his Nature Notebook.

"What a pity. How about putting this one on your wall and drawing a smaller one just like it for your Notebook?"

"Okay," he replied brightly, and off he went.

Michael was in our bedroom all afternoon. When I peeked in on him he seemed disheartened. The gray clouds we could see out the windows didn't help matters. I stared out at the grayness remembering his promise to try to make this new adventure work out.

"You're not worried about anything, are you?" I asked.

"No," he answered, "Just disappointed."

Blueberries

"Okay, good," I replied with a smile. After I gave him a back rub he fell asleep — something I can never remember him doing in the middle of the day.

Some guests left. New ones arrived. Therefore I remade beds and dusted, all the while wishing some needed inspiration for what to cook for supper would come my way. Before I had a chance to open my Fannie Farmer cookbook my needed inspiration came in the form of three generous-sized trout that Pastor and his boys brought by. How glad I am that they are so fond of fishing! Seth, Sarah and, Penelope had also come along. She presented me with what she called a belated house-warming gift — two blueberry pies. Each lively chit-chat I have with Penelope reveals more of what we have in common. I hope we become good friends in the months to come, though I know she is kept very occupied with raising her six children. Their visit was brief.

The dining room was full of hungry guests this evening. One guest in particular, a gregarious gentleman named Mr. Fortesquieu, took Michael's mind off his backache. He is a portly man with an out-of-date handlebar moustache. His clothes, though they look like they've come out of an attic trunk, make a perfect fit. A vigorous conversationalist, he has a deep jovial voice that dominated the others at the table. He was quite appreciative of my "tenderly prepared" fish, raving about the "palatability" of my "exquisite" green salad, impressed with the fact that it was entirely composed of greens we had harvested from the garden. I didn't think the nasturtium petals I sprinkled into the salad would cause such a stir. Don kept his eye on Mr. Fortesquieu, missed his mouth with his fork once, and dropped a piece of cornbread on his lap, he was so riveted. Mr. Fortesquieu's recitations and anecdotes made the whole company lighthearted. He did quiet down some, however, to more slowly consume his blueberry pie — seemingly to savor every mouthful.

Before I could even begin the washing-up, Emma shooed me out of the kitchen. "You go join Michael and Mr. Fortesquieu in the parlor, dear. You ought to get off those feet." I accepted her offer a little hesitantly, for the sake of politeness, though I relished the opportunity.

Michael lit a small fire in the big fireplace to take the rainy day's chill off the room. Darker clouds had rolled in but the crackle of orange flames was quite pleasant. Mr. Fortesquieu carried on with his anecdotes,

Blueberries

asking us some questions that required only general answers. But when the other guests went upstairs, his questions became more pointed — and his expression more serious — though his narrowed eyes still twinkled in the firelight. In response to Mr. Fortesquieu's inquiries, Michael ended up talking all about his last job in marketing, about the conflicting opinions, about his destiny to follow a principle of mediocrity, etc. There was a pause. We all sat in stillness for one brief moment, allowing the crackle of the flames to become the center of attention. Then came Mr. Fortesquieu's startling reply. It swept aside all suavity: "What bumbling buffoons!" he bellowed.

Reflecting on the truth of this statement, Michael, for the first time, saw the humor in his old situation. He laughed a laugh of great relief. Mr. Fortesquieu went on to tell us he was well aware of the silliness that can go on in upper management with those who make a game of business.

"They don't deserve your well-mannered gumption. Losing that job was probably the best thing that ever happed to you. It's beautiful here. I built a small factory beyond the ridge just so I would have the excuse to drive out here part of the year. Unfortunately, most of my income is made in the city."

He turned and gazed back into the firelight; then in a much quieter tone, he said, "Man made the city, you know. God made the country." I felt one of my eyebrows lift. Other than that, I remained unmoved — that is, outwardly. So *he* was the one who owned the canning factory! To cut short the evening's story, Mr. Fortesquieu offered Michael a managerial position at the factory! The job will last for little more than two months, but it will suit him perfectly and the pay is very good. (Blueberries are canned each August, sweet corn in September, and applesauce in October.) This means we will be able to save up some needed cash for the winter months and also have some cash to hire help with the washing.

I knocked on Emma's bedroom door with an energy that surprised me. I wanted to tell her the news. She was sitting in her easy chair with Emily leaning against one arm of the chair and Don against the other — both looking over her shoulder. She was reading to them from one of the volumes of *My Book House*. Outside I heard the rumble of thunder. It wasn't until then that I noticed there was a storm brewing.

"I couldn't send them straight to bed. The thunder is getting close.

Blueberries

Come in, dear," she said, beckoning me over to her. I excitedly announced the good news, and Emma responded with, "Oh, how wonderful, dear. Good-good-good! I love it, I just love it, don't you?" she added with squinted eyes, a radiant smile, and a snuggle for each of her young companions. As it was getting rather late, I bid the children give their grandmother a "Goodnight" and "Thank-you" and to come upstairs with me. Emma blew me a kiss as I closed her door.

While the children and I were passing the parlor, we stopped at the edge of the room to say goodnight to Dad and the portly gentleman. The parlor interview evidently had ended, for at that moment, Michael and the gentleman had their hands clasped in a firm handshake. Then came a flash of lightening and a crack of loud thunder. Emily grabbed hold of me, frightened by the noise. Ordinarily Michael would have whisked his petite Emily up onto his back for a bouncing piggy-back ride up the stairs, to distract her from her fears. Tonight, however, he had to settle for holding her hand.

~

Common boxing turtle — Terrapene carolina
Lowbush blueberry — Vaccinium angustifolium
Nasturtium — Tropaeolum majus

~

Have you ever gone berry picking?

The Rain Is Raining All Around[1]

All this week Michael has left in the morning for the factory in his familiar brown suit — although it now seems to be tight at the shoulders. I guess that's the result of all his painting and haying. I said to him that first morning, "You're filling out."

"So are you," was his retort. Then he whispered in my ear as we stood together at the threshold, "And I find it *quite* alluring!" With that he wiggled his eyebrows as he tipped his hat and went off. Had I been newly wed I would have blushed. Although I hadn't blushed I was a bit lighter on my feet throughout the day.

Because of his work at the factory Michael will not be able to paint the carriage house after all. He overheard a guest comment on how a certain rustic neglect of the country villages contributes to their charm and restful beauty.

Chapter

57

The Rain Is Raining All Around

Therefore he thinks it will in no way hurt business if the carriage house stays as it is until next year.

The children and I have had to spend much of our time indoors because of the rain. It drizzles and persists. Emily has taken to her lessons on knitting. Using thick needles and thick yarn she is already on her way to making her doll a blanket. I have to give myself credit for something clever I did on the day of bread baking. After all our kneading, after Emily's cloverleaf rolls were made, and after Don's bread-dough-tortoise was formed onto a baking pan, I looked at the kitchen table covered with flour and had an idea. Something Miss Mason had written about teaching local geography gave me the idea. I invited the children to turn our floured table into a map of Appleton.[N] With a finger I drew some roads on the flour. I drew Bob's farm, the ridge, the lake, and Blackberry Inn. I invited the children to fill in the rest. They added the brook, the mill, the general store, hay fields, and cow pastures. "What else?" I asked. They added meadows, apple orchards, woods, the church, and the cemetery. In the midst of our activity Emma entered the kitchen, curious about our table decorating. She became quite bubbly when she understood what we were doing. "This is my beloved Appleton? I love it! It's just right. Very good, children! This is Blackberry Inn, isn't it?" Then she used her pinkie finger to add something to the map. She pressed the tip of it into the flour twice beside the Inn and said, "And this is my Don and Emily — perfect!"

"Perfect," I echoed.

~

During this week when the rain has let up a little we have taken some wet naturewalks. I like the smell of a rain-soaked garden. Yesterday, around our feet in the moist grass there were mushrooms. Don wanted to pick some, but having never acquired my father's knowledge of edible mushrooms, I told the children not to touch them. Oh, how self-centered I was as a young lady! On rare occasions, Daddy would ask me to go for a mushroom walk with him, but each time I said that I was too busy. Now I'm sorry I missed the special time I could have had with him, and sorry I considered his knowledge of mushrooms not worth knowing.

The Rain Is Raining All Around

He didn't blame me for not caring about mushrooms, but took walks anyway. Mother was skilled at making buttery dishes with his finds. I did remember, however, that puffballs are not poisonous. We found two the size and color of baseballs. I had the children give them a firm squeeze. I want them to see what changes would transpire. They are tight and springy now, but it won't be long before the balls deflate when touched, releasing the powdery spores formed inside them. Therefore, in a few weeks I must remember to visit them again.

Emily and I gathered quantities of Queen Anne's lace. It covers the countryside in company with goldenrod and black-eyed Susan. "What's that purpley-pink flower?" asked Emily as we walked down the lane in the opposite direction from the cemetery.

"That's the milkweed plant," I answered.

"It doesn't look like milkweed. Where's the fluff?"

"After the flowers have finished blooming, green pods will develop along the stalk. It isn't until late September that the pods open up the way you're used to seeing them," I told her. Don had run ahead, crossed the meadow, and was scouting around in the old apple orchard. He hollered in the usual country fashion:

"Mom, Mom, come, look at this! I found something!"

He was kneeling beside an old stump, looking intently at it. What I saw was a puddle of water resting in the rotten hollow of the stump. "Oh a little puddle, that's cute," I said, baffled, but trying to sound positive.

"No, Mom, look!"

I put my face right up to the puddle beside Don's and saw what he wanted me to see. The water was filled with wigglers. "I know what these are. These are mosquitoes."

"They don't look like mosquitoes," Emily stated.

"Yeah, they don't look like mosquitoes," echoed Don.

I explained to them about the larvae stage and decided that back at home I'd look up more information in Comstock's *Handbook* in order to make a chart of the life cycle of a mosquito. We watched the wigglers twitch for a while. I realize now why Miss Mason advised naturewalks to be a regular thing. Transformations in nature take place daily: buds open into flowers, insect larvae pupate into adults, mushrooms spring up seemingly in hours, flowers turn to fruit or go to seed almost overnight.

The Rain Is Raining All Around

A wet naturewalk will reveal different things than will a sunny walk. But regular walks are the surest way of keeping up with the changes in nature.

When we returned I looked up the poem "Queen Anne's Lace" in my poetry anthology. I think it will make a lovely addition to their Notebooks. I'll have Emily copy one verse a day into her book. I remember my mother reciting the first few lines of it from memory whenever we passed Queen Anne's lace in the meadow. She called it the "wild carrot."

Queen Anne, Queen Anne, has washed her lace
(She chose a summer day)
And hung it in a grassy place
To whiten, if it may.

Queen Anne, Queen Anne, has left it there,
And slept the dewy night;
Then waked, to find the sunshine fair,
And all the meadows white.

Queen Anne, Queen Anne, is dead and gone
(She died a summer's day),
But left her lace to whiten on
Each weed-entangled way!

Don and I read through several poems about insects and settled on one for his Notebook. Big choices should be left up to parents, but I think it makes good sense to give children choices about little things.

The Rain Is Raining All Around

~

Giant puffball — Calvatia gigantea
House mosquito — Culex pipiens
Queen Anne's lace — Daucus carota

~

What can you find on a wet naturewalk?

A Spoon with Roses on the Handle

A young wife and mother named Geraldine came to do the washing and ironing this week. We are so happy to have found her. It would be more accurate to say that she found us, when news got around that we needed help. And since lessons with the children will begin soon I am overjoyed that I'll have some free time to make preparations for the new school year. Geraldine brings with her Celia, her five-month-old baby girl. Emma and I hold her at interludes between the other household duties. What a roly-poly baby she is! Because Geraldine is French, I was reminded of something I had read in *Home Education*, and looked it up to read it again: "French should be acquired as English is, not as a grammar, but as a living speech. To train the ear to distinguish and the lips to produce the French vocables is a valuable part of the education of the senses, and one which can

A Spoon with Roses on the Handle

hardly be undertaken too soon."[1] It was interesting to learn something about how one M. Gouin arrived at his method of teaching, and his reasons for stressing the auditory aspects of learning a foreign language in the same manner in which a young child learns to speak its native tongue. I'd like to talk with Geraldine about the possibility of her sharing her French with Don and Emily by way of this conversation method.°

～

Both Michael and Donald had a birthday this week. Emma made cards for each of them. In Michael's card she had copied a verse and decorated it with pressed cloverleaves:

Here in the country's heart
Where the grass is green
Life is the same sweet life
As it e'er hath been.

Trust in God still lives,
And the bell at morn
Floats with a thought of God
O'er the rising corn.

God comes down in the rain
And the crop grows tall –
This is the country faith,
And the best of all! — Norman Gale

～

A Spoon with Roses on the Handle

Michael likes the birthday present I gave him — argyle socks. It was convenient for me that he had no idea that lately I had been doing my evening knitting for him. Upon reflection he said, "Now the Cyclops can be dressed in good taste."

Don likes his present — a kite. He has been looking out for a good day to fly it. Throughout the sunny morning, puffs of breeze would start and stop, making kite flying seem possible one minute yet near impossible the next. Therefore he asked if he could help his dad with the building of the hen house. After lunch, when the sun would have been beating down on their heads, they took a break from their sawing and hammering, and went to the brook for a swim, Emily of course accompanying them. I remained here to prepare for fall sewing and to take some more time to make more exact proposals for the new school year. Emma led me upstairs to the attic. We dusted off a child's slate easel that she had saved.

"Would Emily like to use it?" she asked.

"She would love to, I'm sure," I said. We also found a box of assorted schoolbooks. Only one or two looked like they'd be useful. I left some miserable readers in the dust, preferring the use of the real books downstairs in the study. I remembered seeing an American history book in the study that I thought would give us some needed information. Some children's biographies would be even better. I'll need to go into town with Michael to search the shelves of the new and used bookshops. I really would like one of those contemporary arithmetic books with colored pictures.

My eye was caught by something outside the low attic window. It was Zorro. Mr. Fortesquieu was snoozing in a lawn chair in the shade. (He comes every weekend to spend his Fridays at the factory and his Saturdays in the garden, returning to the city on Sundays.) That brazen bird was pacing the grass in front of him, even though there was no washing hanging on the lines to attract him.

Emma took a peek out the window, too. "He never married," she informed me.

"Who?" I asked, my attention on Zorro.

"Mr. Fortesquieu, my dear."

It suddenly occurred to me. "You know him well, don't you?"

A Spoon with Roses on the Handle

"He's been coming here for the last six years, every August, ever since he opened up the factory."

"Really?"

"Yes. Every year he asks me to marry him, and every year I decline."

"Really?" I giggled. So did she.

"Yes, really," she confirmed; adding, "he's younger than I am by *years*," with as much emphasis on the word "years" as one could give to it. "I used to think he was just teasing me, cheering me up, making me blush. I do wonder sometimes. Regardless, three husbands are enough for one lifetime, don't you think?"

"He looks lonely."

"Oh, I can assure you, he has plenty of friends and associates in the city, my dear. He comes here for solitude and quiet."

Zorro was no longer pacing the yard. He was perched beside Mr. Fortesquieu's tray of tea. I watched as Zorro pecked at the spoon beside the teacup. Mr. Fortesquieu blinked his eyes in bewilderment, never expecting to see a bird as big as this joining him for tea!

"That rascal! That spoon is from my good set," I cried, whirling on my toes and heading for the stairs.

"Carol, don't run down those circular... You'll never catch up with him!" Emma called after me. I had only gotten halfway down the first flight of stairs when I slipped and tumbled the rest of the way to the second floor.

"Carol, are you all right?" Emma asked, as she slowly made her way down after me.

"How foolish of me," I admitted.

"Never mind, dear. Are you all right?"

"Yes. My dress is torn, that's all." But I wasn't all right. When I was in the bedroom changing my clothes, a wave of cramps came over me. I felt bruised. Dismayed, I lay down on my bed. A summer breeze fluttered the curtains and soothed my perspiring brow as I began praying. When I was finally missed downstairs, Emma came up looking for me. She agreed I should rest in my room, away from the needs of visitors. Then she disappeared to make her health-giving infusion of raspberry leaves so she could bring me up a cup straight away. She was making supper when Michael returned with the children. She must have confided in Michael privately about the afternoon's incident, because in no time Michael was upstairs. As soon as he entered the room tears flew off my cheeks. "Oh Michael," was all I could say.

"I'll get the doctor."

"I'll be all right."

"Carol, I'm going for the doctor. Don't move. I'll be right back."

~

The doctor recommended bed rest, of course. It makes me extra grateful to have Geraldine for the washing — though I don't know how I will get the fall sewing accomplished. And I am uneasy about delaying our trip into the city to order new arithmetic books. Perhaps this lying flat will only be necessary for a few more days. I heard Michael talking with the doctor in the hall. As soon as the doctor was politely seen to the front door, Michael came back upstairs to talk to me. Something was heavy on his mind. He wouldn't look at me. He was upset and unaccustomed to sharing his feelings. Facing the window he confessed, with a mixture of shame and anger, "I shouldn't have brought you here."

"Nonsense," I spoke to the back of his head and with all due respect. "You are not responsible for this. I am. Moving us here has nothing to do with what happened today, either." I had made a reappraisal of the country and was genuine in my reply. "I like it here. I like it here *very* much."

He spun his gaze around to meet mine. "Do you?" He still seemed unconvinced.

"Yes. This will be a perfect place for our baby to grow up," I continued, to reassure him.

"I love you," he told me — this time looking into my eyes deeply.

There was a knock on the door. "Come in," I called. It was Don and Emily.

"Mom, we put my tortoise over by the brook when we went swimming," Don sadly but bravely stated.

"You did the right thing," I told him. "I know it wasn't easy for you." Then I added, "You all need to dress for supper."

Summer

A Spoon with Roses on the Handle

❦

Blackberry Inn was full. A rumble of voices rose up the stairs from the dining room. Most of the rumbling came from the voice of Mr. Fortesquieu. He was probably telling the story about the bandit who stole my spoon with the roses on the handle — although I doubt if he noticed the roses on the handle or spoke of them. Will I ever see it again? They were all laughing. With my head on the pillow watching the clouds out my window, I gave the incident a second thought. I had to admit that it was funny.

After the meal was served Emma brought me a tray of little sandwiches, juicy red tomatoes wedges, creamed corn, another cup of raspberry leaf tea with honey, and a slice of vanilla cake with whipped cream topped with freshly grated coconut. I felt utterly pampered. Michael and the children were taking charge of the washing up in the kitchen. When Emma asked me how I felt, I told her that my cramps had subsided.

"Oh good, dear. I'll let Michael know. I'm so glad. It *is* very good, dear, but you mustn't get up. Now you get your bed rest, as the doctor said." This was spoken cheerfully while pressing a hand firmly on my shoulder that personified the meaning of the word *stay*. Her commandment reminded me of that winter's day in Dora's kitchen when I was the one doing the ordering about, though not as tactfully. She took the tray when I was finished and bid me goodnight. I thought she looked tired. I wish I hadn't been so impetuous, I thought to myself as I lay back, staring at the ceiling.

As soon as I heard the children run up the stairs I sat up in bed in time for their knock. Emily entered first with Don following. Emily was holding something behind her back with both hands.

"Do you want the big one first, or the little one?" she asked.

"Oh, the big one, I think."

"This is the big one," she said, handing me a bouquet of wild purple asters and some calico asters that she had probably picked from the roadside or the edge of the meadow. The last flowers of the season, I thought to myself. I shall cherish them. Then I told her that the name aster means "star."

"Do they look like stars?" I asked. She nodded.

A Spoon with Roses on the Handle

"And this is the little one." Her round fist held a combination of fuzzy rabbit-foot clover and some yellow hops clover.

"Thank you, Emily. This little bouquet will fit well in an egg cup," I told her. Here is a verse that matches my sentiments exactly:

I never see a young hand hold
The starry bunch of white and gold,
But something warm and fresh will start
About the region of my heart. — Eliza Cook[2]

⁓

The combination of flowers gave me an idea. "Hand me the field guide from the shelf," I told Don. "Come closer, children." First I opened to a pair of pages with all the plants in the pea (or legume) family. Don and Emily recognized most of them. I pointed out the common name and scientific name. The scientific name (or Latin name) always uses two words, *genus* and *species*. All the clover on one page had the same first name *trifolium* and a different second name. I showed them more examples of these Latin names throughout the book. "We can go back and add the scientific names to all your Nature Notebook drawings," I said. Don was mildly interested. Then I made a mental note: "Tomorrow," I told myself, "I must remember to tell the children to check on the puffballs. I think, by now, they ought to be powdery."

After pajamas were on and teeth brushed I read to them — Don on one side of me and Emily on the other. Don brought me a volume of *My Book House*. We read about Henri Fabre and his fairyland of science.[3] What an insect lover Fabre was and what a passionate observer of the tiny creatures! The illustrations in the book showed insects playing musical instruments among tall blades of grass.

"There are grasshoppers all around the yard, just like the one in this picture," said Don, my insect buff.

"The hens will have a feast then," I said.

"When are we getting our chickens?" asked Emily.

A Spoon with Roses on the Handle

"Dad and I are almost done with the hen house," reported Don.

"It won't be long now, " I mused.

"Oh, good." Emily replied. I was just about to begin another story when we heard three knocks on the door, and Michael walked in. Between the window curtains a thin line of the horizon was an incandescent violet. The rest of the sky was a hazy dark blue.

"It's getting late, children," said their dad. " Come with me. Time for our Bible reading and bed."

"Did you light a small fire downstairs?" I interrupted, although I thought it strange, since the evening was so warm.

"No."

"I smell smoke. Don't you?"

"It's probably just Mr. Fortesquieu's cigars," Michael admitted. "He passed out a few of his best Havanas." Giving my question another thought he turned to face the window to the back yard. "Hmm, perhaps it's coming from outside," he said, and stepped toward the window to look out. Then he enlarged his deep voice in a manner that startled us.

"Jiminy Cricket! The outhouse is on fire!"

"What?" I shrieked.

The children sprang to the window. I got up cautiously and looked out, too. I couldn't miss this. And what a sight! Bright yellow flames were belching out of the little crescent moon of a vent hole. Little gray puffs of smoke rose from all sides of it. There was a commotion downstairs. There were calls and shouts. Gentlemen guests were carrying pails of water to the scene.

Michael stepped away from the window and with knuckles under chin and a pensive gaze to the floor, he paced the room, thinking out loud, as though he were solving a mystery in the manner of Mr. Holmes. "It must have been the cigar Mr. Fortesquieu gave me. Yes, that's it! I accidentally dropped it on the Sears catalog when I... the bathroom downstairs was occupied you see, I... I never thought... It had to have been ashes from the cigar."

Upon hearing his deliberations I threw back my head and burst out an unladylike belly-laugh. It was the most satisfying laugh of the year. "Never mind," I said with a sly smile, "Good riddance. Let it burn."

A Spoon with Roses on the Handle

"Yeah," he said, putting his arm around me, joining me at the window. "Let it burn."

~

Calico aster — Aster lateriflorus
Grasshopper ("Carolina locust") — Dissosteira carolina
Palmate hop clover — Trifolium aureum
Purple-stemmed aster — Aster puniceus
Rabbit-foot clover — Trifolium arvense

~

The End

Appendices

Supplement

There are so many helpful pages for the mother in Charlotte Mason's *Home Education* (written in 1886) that I decided to include a small sampling here. It will give you a peek at what Carol was reading. She didn't attempt to apply everything she was learning from *Home Education* during her very first year of home teaching. Applying *some* was an excellent beginning. She had the courage to be experimental.

The pages of *Home Education* gave Carol a philosophy and method on which to draw. To have an aim and a direction, even if accomplishments are small at the start, is far better than to drift along in insecurity and confusion, relying only upon snippets of advice from well-meaning friends. Even with clear guidance such as that found in *Home Education*, home teaching may still be a struggle. Please understand that a new home teacher goes through a transition period. It takes time to adjust to new thinking, new ways of doing things, to summon up the courage to break from old ways that haven't worked well in the past with one's children — especially if those ways are widely accepted in our society.

Carol put her trust in a method that appealed to her. She was careful to attempt no more than she felt she could handle at any given time. She couldn't fully realize the ideal educational environment presented in *Home Education*. She had to be content with what she was able to do, while acknowledging room for improvement. In her subsequent year of home teaching, at Blackberry Inn, she proposed to add other subjects: setting up a time for regular Picture Study, the reading of biographies, and the introduction of a foreign language.

Time taken to read and appreciate the books in the Blackberry Inn library insured her own mental growth. The home teacher mustn't let herself stagnate. It was Carol's duty to take part in Mother Culture to keep her heart and mind freshly stirred up for her task at hand. I hope I have contributed to the "stirring up" of your heart and mind in the pages of *Pocketful of Pinecones*.

FROM CHAPTER ONE:

A. *Vocabulary*
"When a child is reading, he should not be teased with questions as to the meaning of what he has read, the signification of this word or that... It is not in the least consequence that they should be able to give the meaning of every word they read. A knowledge of meanings, that is, an ample and correct vocabulary, is only arrived at in one way — by the habit of reading. A child unconsciously gets the meaning of a new word from the context, if not the first time he meets with it, then the second or the third; but he is on the look-out, and will find out for himself the sense of any expression he does not understand."(p. 228)

Supplement

FROM CHAPTER TWO:

B. *A Child's Reading*
"A child has not begun his education until he has acquired the habit of reading to himself, with interest and pleasure, books fully on a level with his intelligence. I am speaking now of his lesson-books, which are all too apt to be written in a style of insufferable twaddle, probably because they are written by persons who have never chanced to meet a child... Children can take in ideas and principles... as quickly and as clearly as we do ourselves (perhaps more so); but detailed processes, lists and summaries [of the usual textbook] blunt the edge of a child's delicate mind. Therefore, the selection of their first lesson-books is a matter of grave importance, because it rests with these to give children the idea that knowledge is supremely attractive and that reading is delightful. Once the habit of reading his lesson-books with delight is set up in a child, his education is not completed, but — ensured; he will go on for himself in spite of the obstructions which school too commonly throws in his way. (p. 229)

C. *Books Written by the Naturalist*
"The real use of naturalists' books at this stage is to give the child delightful glimpses into the world of wonders he lives in, to reveal the sort of things to be seen by curious eyes, and fill him with desire to make discoveries for himself. There are many to be had, all pleasant reading, many of them written by scientific men, and yet requiring little or no scientific knowledge for their enjoyment." (p. 64)

FROM CHAPTER SEVEN:

D. *A Seed of Sympathy*
"There is one thing the mother will allow herself to do as interpreter between Nature and the child, but that not oftener than once a week or once a month, and with look and gesture of delight rather than with flow of improving words — she will point out to the child some touch of especial loveliness in colouring or grouping in the landscape or in

the heavens. One other thing she will do, but very rarely, and with tender... reverence... : she will point to some lovely flower or gracious tree, not only as a beautiful work, but a beautiful *thought* of God, in which we may believe He finds continual pleasure, and which He is pleased to see his human children rejoice in. Such a seed of sympathy with the Divine thought sown in the heart of the child is worth many of the sermons the man may listen to hereafter, much of the 'divinity' he may read."(pp. 79-80)

FROM CHAPTER TWELVE:

E. *A Schedule Of Shorter Lessons*
"...[L]et us look in at a home schoolroom managed upon sound principles. In the first place, there is a time-table, written out fairly, so that the child knows what he has to do and how long each lesson is to last. This idea of definite work to be finished in a given time is valuable to the child, not only as training him, in habits of order, but in diligence; he learns that one time is *not* as good as another; that there is no right time left for what is not done in its own time; and this knowledge alone does a great deal to secure the child's *attention* to his work. Again, the lessons are short, seldom more than twenty minutes in length for children under eight; and this, for two or three reasons. The sense that there is not much time for his sums or his reading, keeps the child's wits on the alert and helps to fix his attention; he has time to learn just so much of any one subject as it is good for him to take in at once.; and if the lessons be judiciously alternated — sums first, say, while the brain is quite fresh, then writing, or reading — some more or less mechanical exercise by way of a rest; and so on, the program varying a little from day to day, but the same principle throughout — a 'thinking' lesson first, and a 'painstaking' lesson to follow, — the child gets through his morning lessons without any sign of weariness." (p. 142)

Supplement

FROM CHAPTER EIGHTEEN:

F. *Narration*
"Children narrate by nature. — Narrating is an *art*, like poetry-making or painting, because it is *there*, in every child's mind, waiting to be discovered, and is not the result of any process of disciplinary education. A creative fiat calls it forth, 'Let him narrate'; and the child narrates, fluently, copiously, in ordered sequence, with fit and graphic details, with a just choice of words, without verbosity or tautology, so soon as he can speak with ease. This amazing gift with which normal children are born is allowed to lie fallow in their education. Bobbie will come home with a heroic narrative of a fight he has seen between 'Duke' and a dog in the street. It is wonderful! He has seen everything, and he tells everything with splendid vigor in the true epic vein; but so ingrained is our contempt for children that we see nothing in this but Bobbie's foolish childish way! Whereas here, if we have eyes to see and grace to build, is the ground-plan of his education." (p. 231)

FROM CHAPTER TWENTY-ONE:

G. *Laying the Groundwork for Further Education*
"...There is no part of a child's education more important than that he should lay, by his own observation, a wide basis of *facts* towards scientific knowledge in the future. He must live hours daily in the open air, and, as far as possible, in the country; must look and touch and listen; must be quick to note, *consciously*, every peculiarity of habit or structure, in beast, bird, or insect; the manner of growth and fructification of every plant. He must be accustomed to ask *why* — Why does the wind blow? Why does the river flow? Why is a leaf-bud sticky?" (p. 264)

"The *method* of this sort of instruction is shown in *Evenings at Home*, where 'Eyes and No-eyes' go for a walk. No-eyes comes home bored; he has seen nothing, been interested in nothing; while Eyes is all agog to discuss a hundred things that have interested him. As I have already tried to point out, to get this sort of instruction for himself is simply the *nature* of a child: the business of the parent is to afford him abundant and varied opportunities, and to direct his observations, so that, knowing little of the principles of scientific classification, he is, unconsciously, furnishing himself with the materials for such classification... the future of man or woman depends very largely on the store of real knowledge gathered, and the habits of intelligent observation acquired, by the child." (p. 265)

FROM CHAPTER THIRTY-THREE:

H. *Reading Aloud*
"He should have practice, too, in reading aloud, for the most part, in the books he is using for his term's work. These should include a good deal of poetry, to accustom him to the delicate rendering of shades of meaning, and especially to make him aware that words are beautiful in themselves, that they are a source of pleasure, and are worthy of our honor; and that a beautiful word deserves to be beautifully said, with a certain roundness of tone and precision of utterance. Quite young children are open to this sort of teaching, conveyed, not in a lesson, but by a word now and then." (p. 227)

FROM CHAPTER THIRTY-NINE:

I. *Watching*
"Children should be encouraged to *watch* patiently and quietly, until they learn something of the habits and history of bee, ant, wasp, spider, hairy caterpillar, dragon-fly, and whatever of larger growth comes in their way. 'The creatures never have any habits while I am looking!' a little girl in some story-book is made to complain: but that was her fault; the bright keen eyes with which children are blest were made to see, and see into, the doings of creatures too small for the unaided observation of older people." (p. 57)

Supplement

FROM CHAPTER FORTY:

J. *History*
"...they [the old chroniclers] purl along pleasantly as a forest brook, tell you 'all about it,' stir your heart with the story of a great event, amuse you with pageants and shows, make you intimate with the great people, and friendly with the lowly. They are just the right thing for the children whose eager souls want to get at the living people behind the words of the history book, caring nothing at all about progress, or statutes, or about anything but the persons, for whose action history is, to the child's mind, no more than a convenient stage. A child who has been carried through a single old chronicle in this way has a better foundation for an historical training than if he knew all the dates and names and facts that ever were crammed for examination." (p. 282)

FROM CHAPTER FORTY-FOUR:

K. *Composition*
"Composition comes by nature. — In fact, lessons on *'composition'* should follow the model of that famous essay on 'Snakes in Ireland' — 'There are none.' For children under nine, the question of composition resolves itself into that of narration, varied by some such simple exercise as to write a part and narrate a part, or write the whole account of a walk they have taken, a lesson they have studied, or of some simple matter that they know. Before they are ten, children who have been in the habit of using books will write good, vigorous English with ease and freedom; that is, if they have not been hampered by instructions. It is well for them not even to learn rules for the placing of full stops and capitals until they notice how these things occur in their books. Our business is to provide children with material in their lessons and *leave the handling of such material to themselves*. If we would believe it, composition is as natural as jumping and running to children who have been allowed due use of books. They should narrate in the first place, and they will compose, later, readily enough; but they should not be taught 'composition.'" (p. 247)

Supplement

FROM CHAPTER FORTY-NINE:

L. *Picture Study*
"When children have begun regular lessons... [the] study of pictures should not be left to chance, but they should take one artist after another, term by term, and study quietly some half-dozen reproductions of his work in the course of a term... something definite remains with a child after his studies... We cannot measure the influence that one or another artist has upon the child's sense of beauty, upon his power of seeing, as in a picture, the common sights of life; he is enriched more than we know in having really looked at even a single picture." (pp. 308-309)

FROM CHAPTER FIFTY-THREE:

M. *Bible Reading*
"A word about the reading of the Bible. I think we make a mistake in burying the text under our endless comments and applications. Also, I doubt if the picking out of individual verses, and grinding these into the child until they cease to have any meaning for him, is anything but a hindrance to the spiritual life. The Word is full of vital force, capable of applying itself. A seed, light as thistledown, wafted into the child's soul, will take root downwards and bear fruit upwards. What is required of us is, that we should implant a *love* of the Word; that the most delightful moments of the child's day should be those in which his mother [or father] reads for him, with sweet sympathy and holy gladness in voice and eyes, the beautiful stories of the Bible; and now and then in the reading will occur one of those convictions, passing from the soul of the mother to the soul of the child, in which is the life of the Spirit. Let the child grow, so that,

> *'New thoughts of God, new hopes of heaven,'*

are a joy to him, too; things to be counted first amongst the blessings of a day. Above all, do not read the Bible *at* the child; do not let any words of the Scriptures be occasions for gibbeting his faults. It is the office of the Holy Ghost to convince of sin; and He is able to use the Word for this purpose, without risk of that hardening of the heart in which our clumsy dealings too often result." (pp. 348-349)

FROM CHAPTER FIFTY-SEVEN:

N. *Local Geography*
"It is probable that a child's own neighborhood will give him opportunities to learn the meaning of hill and dale, pool and brook, watershed, the current, bed, banks, tributaries of a brook, the relative positions of villages and towns; and all this local geography he must be able to figure roughly on a plan done with chalk on a rock, or with walking-stick in the gravel, perceiving the relative distances and situations of the places he marks." (p. 78)

FROM CHAPTER FIFTY-EIGHT:

O. *French*
"Whatever may be said of M. Gouin's methods, the steps by which he arrives at them are undoubtedly scientific.... The little child, which at the age of two years utters nothing but meaningless exclamations, at the age of three finds itself in possession of a complete language. How does it accomplish this?... The organ of language... is not the eye: it is the ear. The eye is made for colours, and not for sounds and words... [M. Gouin] knew everybody's 'Method,' learned the whole dictionary through, and found at the end that he did not know *one word* of German 'as she is spoke.'

He returned to France, after a ten months' absence, and found that his little nephew — whom he had left, a child of two and a half, not yet able to talk — had in the interval done what his uncle had signally failed to do. [He writes:] 'What! I thought; 'this child and I have been working for the same time, each at a language. He, playing round his mother, running after flowers, butterflies and birds, without weariness, without apparent effort, without even being conscious of his work, is able to say all he thinks, express all he sees, understand all he hears; and when he began his work, his intelligence was yet a futurity, a glimmer, a hope. And I, versed in the sciences, versed in philosophy, armed with a powerful will, gifted with a powerful memory... have arrived at nothing, or practically nothing!'

'The linguistic science of the college has deceived me, has misguided me. The classical method, with its grammar, its dictionary, and its translations, is a delusion. To surprise Nature's secret, I must watch this child.'"(pp. 304-306)

SOME EXTRA QUOTATIONS NOT REFERENCED TO PARTICULAR CHAPTERS:

Observing Birds
There is a lovely section on bird-watching, subtitled more specifically "Bird Stalking," on pages 89 through 92, after the paragraphs on scouting. Did you know that it was a Charlotte Mason-trained governess that sparked the idea for the scouting movement? Sir Robert Baden-Powell credits Charlotte Mason for suggesting that the advice in his book *Aids to Scouting* (a little handbook for soldiers) be made applicable for children.

All Lessons
On page 177 of *Home Education* Charlotte Mason lists four tests by which the children's lessons should be measured. Children's lessons should:

a) Provide material for their mental growth,

b) Exercise the several powers of their minds,

c) Furnish them with fruitful ideas,

d) Afford them knowledge, really interesting, of the kind that the child may recall as a man with profit and pleasure.

⁓

Supplement

A Childhood

Before applying these tests to the various subjects in which children are commonly instructed, Charlotte Mason reminds us of six points which she endeavored to establish in the first part of *Home Education*:

a) That the knowledge most valuable to the child is that which he gets with his own eyes and ears and fingers (under direction) in the open air.

b) That the claims of the schoolroom should not be allowed to encroach on the child's right to long hours daily for exercise and investigation.

c) That the child should be taken daily, if possible, to scenes — moor or meadow, park, common, or shore — where he may find new things to examine, and so observation should be directed to flower or boulder, gathering the common information which is the basis of scientific knowledge.

d) That play, vigorous, healthful play, is, in its turn, fully as important as lessons as regards both bodily health and brain-power.

e) That the child, though under supervision, should be left much to himself — both that he may go to work in his own way on the ideas he receives, and also that he may be the more open to natural influences.

f) That the happiness of the child is the condition of this progress; that his lessons should be joyous, and that occasions of friction in the schoolroom are greatly to be deprecated.

~

Home Education is Volume One of a series of six books in the Charlotte Mason series. This series of Miss Mason's original writings is published by The Charlotte Mason Research & Supply Company, a company run by my husband and myself, dedicated since 1988 to sharing Charlotte Mason's philosophy and method with today's parents. Miss Mason's books are typically printed and sold as a set, but we do have a limited number of copies of Volume One available while the supply lasts.

Supplement

Your comments and opinions are welcome. You can reach me by writing:

Karen Andreola
Charlotte Mason R & S, Co.
P.O. Box 758
Union, Maine, 04862

~

Look for related material on our website: charlottemason.com. Here you will also find a description of the book, *A Charlotte Mason Companion – Personal Reflections of the Gentle Art of Learning*. This non-fiction book represents my first eight years of research and experience in home educating my own children by way of what I call "the gentle art of learning." There are numerous chapters on a variety of subjects. Some chapter headings are: The Atmosphere of Home; The Happiness of Habit; How We Use Whole Books; Narration – The Art of Knowing; Hero-Admiration as a Factor in Education; Picture Study; Music Appreciation; Approach to Poetry; Shakespeare – A Mother's Secret Resource; Charles Dickens from a Mother's Point of View; History; and Mother Culture. If you do not have a computer we will gladly send you a brochure.

In the brochure or on our website you will find a description of the back issues of *Parents' Review – A Magazine for Home Training and Culture*, the magazine we published for six years. The issues are more often sold by the year, as a set. However, if you would like a copy of the issue of the *Parents' Review* that contains the article "The Fairyland of Science" (the story that was being read to Don and Emily in the last chapter), please send $5.00 to the address above. Specify "last issue" with your order.

Suggested Reading

In early June the open roads of Maine are lit up in purple with patches of wild lupines. It is against the law to pick them. These large hardy flowers are good for tourism because they lend a sort of storybook charm to the countryside. Because I had read *Miss Rumphius* to my children while we lived in Maryland, when we moved to Maine I recognized the flowers at once, even though I had not been expecting to see them. Now every June I look forward to these blossoms. I later learned that the story *Miss Rumphius* is based on the life of a real woman, who really did, in 1948, cast her lupine seeds along the roadsides. The book was written and illustrated by Barbara Cooney, who up until 1999 (she has passed away) summered every year on the coast of Maine.

~

Suggested Reading

Snowflake Bently, by Jacqueline Brigs Martin, is a picture book about a man with scientific vision, who thought of snow crystals as small miracles and endeavored to photograph them. According to a winter issue of *Northern New England Journey*, Mr. Wilson Alwyn Bently (1865-1931) was homschooled until the age of fourteen. He then received a high school education and spent his adult life as a dairy farmer. But his passion for understanding the mysteries of precipitation made him a pioneer of photomicrography. He photographed more than 5,000 individual snowflakes.

~

The little stories by Beatrice Potter (1866-1943) are meant to be held in a little child's hand. They are fanciful but lovely because a lover of nature wrote them. Her watercolor illustrations are the result of her close association with the creatures of the countryside.

~

Thornton Burgess (1874-1965) was "the most widely read author of children's nature stories in the United States from 1910 to 1950," according to Frances B. Meigs, in her book, *My Grandfather, Thornton W. Burgess* — a signed copy of which I was given for my birthday! Many homeschooled children are being raised on old books and they are finding great delight in Burgess' classic stories today.

~

The country veterinarian James Herriot writes true stories about animals for young children (and adults), based on his own experiences.

~

Factual information on God's creatures can be found in Christian

Suggested Reading

Liberty's *Nature Readers*, Books 3 and 4. I like the fact that the information is presented in a writing style that is palatable to children. These inexpensive readers are reprints of old texts.

~

A picture book that introduces children to the botanical artist Pierre Joseph Redoute (1759-1840) is titled, *Redoute — The Man who Painted Flowers*, by Carolyn Croll. Botanical drawings became unpopular when photography stepped into the scientific picture. Today, however, there is a resurgence of interest in botanical drawing, in the style of accurate drawings of plants on a background of white. You'll find botanical prints for sale in art print shops.

~

 *The Story of John J. Audubon* (1785-1851), by Joan Howard, is a chapter book that is, unhappily, out of print. Perhaps your local library has this, or a different biography on the life of this amazing man, whose goal was to draw and document as many American birds as he could find. When no American publisher would agree to print his book, he went to England, where his pictures were so admired that they became a sensation. His *Birds of America* contains 435 life-sized engravings painted with his water colors.

~

Ernest Thompson Seton (1860-1946) wrote the first Boy Scout manual. He is most famous for his animal tales, which are based on his personal observations. *Lives of the Hunted* is the book Don reads in *Pocketful of Pinecones*. There are at times sad endings to his funny stories, as Mr. Seton often includes the true and natural deaths of the creatures he studied with such dedication.

~

Suggested Reading

Country Diary of an Edwardian Lady by Edith Holden (1871-1920) is back in print. Three cheers! I highly recommend it. When I came across it more than ten years ago on a "sale table" at a big book store, I immediately recognized it as a beautiful example of the kind of Nature Notebook that Charlotte Mason advised all her students to endeavor to create. Our attempts at recording what we find in the woods and roadsides will most likely not be as successful as that of Edith Holden, who attended art school as a young lady. The book is, however, inspiring. I always prefer to spend my money on *inspiring* books. The video version is calm and relaxing. It provides film footage of the same plants and animals featured on the pages of the book. In it an actress plays Edith Holden taking naturewalks and writing and painting in her diary.

~

Playful ideas for growing vegetables and flowers in the backyard, "kid-style," can be found in *Sunflower Houses — Garden Discoveries for Children of All Ages,* by Sharon Lovejoy.

~

What happens to a field that lies fallow? *How The Forest Grew* by William Jaspersohn describes the gradual transformation of a cleared farm field into a dense forest. It has black and white pen drawings.

~

The Passionate Observer — Writings from the World of Nature, by Jean Henri Fabre (1823-1915), provides sample writings of the Frenchman who led the study of living entomology. Before him, nonliving specimens were examined in laboratories. Fabre observed the habits and mannerisms of insects as they lived in their own environment. He never lost his zest for the insect world and its multitudinous mysteries. This book is for older readers.

Suggested Reading

∽

Ring of Bright Water, by Gavin Maxwell, recounts the author's experience living in Scotland among the unspoiled landscape of the West Highland seaboard in a lonely, roadless cottage. After his dog died, he brought an otter cub back from the marches and made it his pet. It turned out that this otter was a creature unknown to science. Later the scientific world gave this species of otter Maxwell's own name. This autobiography is for high school students and adults. A British film was made of the story some years back.

∽

The zoning laws of some suburban neighborhoods allow for the keeping of a very small number of hens, but not roosters. I found *Chickens in Your Backyard* to be a good beginners guide. On a summer evening the authors, Rick and Gail Luttmann, sit back and watch their chickens instead of television. They tell us that this is much more interesting.

∽

A story that savors the country life is *Dune Boy — The Early Years of a Naturalist*, by Edwin Way Teale. The author spent his boyhood summers in the northern Indiana dune country on his grandparents' farm. This is a nostalgic account of the days before WWI. Mr. Teale was awarded a Pulitzer Prize for a nature-writing series. More sophisticated writing than *Farmer Boy*, by Laura Ingalls Wilder and just as charming, this lesser-known book is a good one for older boys and adults.

∽

Character First is excellent crossover material written by Christians for use in any classroom or workplace. Nature stories are used to demonstrate

Suggested Reading

a range of positive character traits. For a brochure, contact Don Gilbert, 524 E. Timberwood Creek, Spokane, WA 99298.

⌒

I recommend *A Girl of the Limberlost*, a novel by Gene Stratton Porter about a teen-age girl who loves nature. The setting is the rural Midwest in the early 1900s. It was made into a film by Wonderworks.

⌒

Following is a list of some other fictional stories that have an aspect of nature in them. We have enjoyed reading all of these stories in our home over the years.

Aesop's Fables
Bambi and *Bambi's Children* by Felix Salten
Black Beauty by Anna Sewell
Charlotte's Web by E. B. White
Cricket in Times Square by George Selden
Gentle Ben by Walt Morey
Heidi by Johanna Spyri
The Incredible Journey by Sheila Burnford
Julie of the Wolves by Jean Craighead George
Island of the Blue Dolphins by Scott O'Dell
Jungle Book by Rudyard Kipling
Lassie Come-Home by Eric Knight
Miss Hickory by Carolyn Sherwin Bailey
Misty of Chincoteague by Marguerite Henry
My Side of the Mountain by Jean Craighead George
Paddle to the Sea by Holling Clancy Holling
Pago by Holling Clancy Holling
Rascal by Sterling North
Robinson Crusoe by Daniel Defoe
The Secret Garden by Frances Hodgson Burnett
Swiss Family Robinson by Johann Wyss

Suggested Reading

The Water Babies by Charles Kingsley
The Wheel on the School by Meindert DeJong
Wind in the Willows by Kenneth Grahame

~

Although Anna Comstock's *Handbook of Nature Study* is an old book, it is still in print. Miss Comstock (1854-1930) was a professor of nature study at Cornell University. Carol refers to Comstock's *Handbook* often. It is a teacher's resource for kindergarten through grade twelve. Over eight hundred pages, it is a sort of personalized nature encyclopedia that includes observation questions and Miss Comstock's helpful suggestions for fieldwork.

~

Keeping a Nature Journal is a much newer book by Clare Walker Leslie and Charles E. Roth that teaches simple methods of capturing what you see outdoors in sketches and in words. It is filled with illustrated examples and tips so that your journal will represent your personal experience.

~

Most of the writings of Jacques-Yves Cousteau are out of print. We have a few books in the series, *The Undersea Discoveries of Jacques-Yves Cousteau*. The experiences of the crew of the *Calypso* are worth reading and searching for in your local used book shop. His love of the sea creatures he studied comes through in his writing. The experiences he shares are fascinating to children.

~

Field guides are indispensable for studying the natural world. The Audubon Society publishes the guides we use. When my children were very young we had guides by Golden Books. You can also purchase recordings of bird songs so that you can identify which birds are making the many beautiful sounds you hear in your neighborhood.

~

You are sure to come across many more books (than those above) with a nature theme that appeal to you. Geology, astronomy, botany, zoology, entomology, oceanography, ornithology, ecology, physics, etc. all have their roots in rudimentary nature study. The study of science does not have to be dry and boring. Rather, it can be inspiring. When you fill your homeschool with the writings and lives of people who were enthusiastic about what they observed and the knowledge they gained, you will find that their enthusiasm is catching.

Afterword

One of my favorite pastimes with my young children was to hold their chubby hands and walk with them through the neighborhood to see what we could notice about the season. Borrowing from the newness of their experience, I took joy. Even during their high school years we found time for naturewalks — time to admire what each season brought our way.

~

I earnestly hope that *Pocketful of Pinecones* has inspired you, at least to a small degree, to spend more time outdoors, to keep your eyes open for the nature in your neck of the woods or in your town, *and* to keep a record of it.

Afterword

May you and your family have the pleasure of finding things out for yourselves, of investigating God's marvelous creation.

It's not necessary to study half a dozen things in one afternoon. One or two bits of nature a week is probably more manageable. One thirty-minute naturewalk a week is a good beginning. Spring will offer more to see than any other season. In fact, nature in spring can be hard to keep up with. On a summer's day you may find nothing new, but changes may be observed in flora and fauna seen earlier in the season. Take your time. Nature will educate you in your leisure. Do make a point, however, to appoint a specific time in your schedule for this leisure. I think you will find it a refreshing study.

Pocketful of Pinecones took nearly two years to write because I write by inches. The majority of my life's work is dedicated to my family. While I was away from my desk I would play out various scenes in my head. A few experiences or reminiscences from friends provided material at times. For instance, when a church member told me about the nasty rooster she had in 1947, she gave me the idea for Tailgate. But as all ideas need a time of germination, I still had to rely upon my own experience with nature and teaching children and then work the ideas into the story. The chick stuck on Reliable's tongue in the story is a true incident described to me.

As a family we have observed all the nature mentioned in this story. Careful attention was given to scientific details, but I cannot claim absolute accuracy. For example, red cardinals do not typically live in upper New England in the winter. They have been spotted in winter in lower New England only recently. I couldn't resist including them in my story because you may be able to spot them in your neighborhood. Milkweed blooms in July, and has green pods by August. In my story, Emily notices flowers in August. Other than the cardinal and the milkweed I was very careful. The appearances of certain blooms do differ in parts of New England by weeks anyway. Since many of you who are reading this book live outside of New England you will be following nature's time clock in your own part of the country. You will be following the appearance of your own sets of the wildflowers, insects, birds, etc., that are indigenous to your own region of the country. For those of you who do reside in New England you will be able to find most of the nature

Afterword

observed in *Pocketful of Pinecones* pictured in the National Audubon Society's *Field Guide to New England*.

In our more than twenty years of marriage we have lived in city, town, suburb, and country. When we lived in London we lived in a third floor apartment. We had no backyard, so my little girls and I often walked to a park or playground. We have had to move a lot. Whenever we lived in the suburbs we would scour the backyard and neighborhood for whatever it contained. I would plant fall bulbs, even if we were renting, so that spring would greet us with at least a small sampling of flowers.

~

Here in Maine

~

Presently we live in the woods of Maine. When I turned forty-one my dream of buying a house in the country came true. Around the corner is Rock Maple Farm where maple syrup is made. My son helped collect sap in March and rode on a wooden sled drawn by oxen around the trees, through the mud. We stepped into the sugar house to see the sap boiling. The evaporator is heated with wood. Our host served us some hot maple syrup over a dish of vanilla ice cream.

Our daughters have raked lowbush blueberries. Their backs were sore but they pressed on. I gave it a one-minute try. That was enough. The view of the lake from the blueberry fields on the ridge is truly spectacular. The valley is snug and picturesque with its lake, farms, and white church steeple. The homemade blueberry pies served in the restaurants here are filled with hundreds of itty-bitty, bursting-with-flavor, lowbush blueberries. A recent study claims them to be the most cancer-fighting fruit there is.

The cemetery at the end of our dirt road is actually on our property. It is deeded to the town. The earliest birth recorded on a gravestone is 1803. Some of the names in this book were taken from certain gravestones. The name Emma Cook, however, is that of my own great-grandmother's mother, who outlived three husbands. It was her first husband (not her last) who was a descendant of Francis Cook of the Plymouth settlement. She ran a tourist home on Route Nine in New Jersey — the old road to Atlantic City. My mother took me to visit the house. It is presently used for a Victorian gift shop, and is now painted two shades of pink. The outhouse was brought closer to the house and it is also painted pink. I bought a teacup there as a souvenir.

My mother remembers staying in the house as a young lady and showed me two old black and white photographs of all the cousins sitting on the porch. The house is close to the seaside. She remembers that her mother had to empty chamber pots every morning. That was as late as the 1940s. My great-great grandmother was a puritanical wife of a pastor (her last husband). A "Tsk, tsk," was heard by her if she caught anyone in the neighborhood with washing on the line on a Sunday. But she was kind and cheerful to everyone and worked hard. She loved cooking for people. My mother remembers her large platters of eggs — compliments of the chickens out back.

Speaking of chickens, we have a small flock of laying hens, New Hampshire Reds. They roam the lawn, scratch everywhere, and make a mess of the flower garden with their sunbathing and dust baths. They follow at my heels, across the lawn and straight into their coop when I sing to them because they know I carry sunflower seeds for their dessert. Our cats are lazy and don't care for mice. But our largest hen, Fanny, is a mouser. When a pile of cord wood was finally picked up and neatly stacked, there was a mess of wood chips in the grass needing to be raked. Fanny found a baby mouse in the wood chips and ran away with the pink hairless creature dangling in her beak. "There is never just one baby mouse," I said to my son. Sure enough, moments later she returned for a second and third course. A week later we heard Fanny clucking out a scream in the garage. She had cornered a full-grown mouse and had pecked it bloody. My daughter whisked the mouse away into the woods. She was disgusted. I was, too, but I couldn't help snicker at the same time. (These kinds of realistic scenes are typically not included in storybooks.) One apprehensive hen fussed at the sliding glass door for over an hour when it came near the time to lay her first egg. Did she wish to make herself comfortable in the living room? We found her later, quieted down, in the garage. She was sitting on the seat of our riding mower. Someone

Afterword

who called her a naughty bird had to remove her from the mower three times. Since making a nest in one corner of the garage (ignoring the nesting box in the coop), she is content and more relaxed about the experience. We placed a ceramic egg in her nesting box to entice her and so she won't feel robbed. She still prefers to lay elsewhere. I now have a better understanding of the character Jemima Puddle-Duck.

One morning in spring my son took me over to the chicken coop to show me something. A tiny garden spider had built a wheel of a web in one of the hexagonal chicken wire spaces. It was then that I decided to put it in my story.

We keep an old narrow carriage road maintained so we can walk down to the brook. The bridge is gone but there is a pile of large rocks in its place. When the water runs over these rocks it makes a lovely sound. Last spring a beaver dam appeared upstream. It has slowed the brook quit a bit. We haven't spotted the beaver but the children have walked on top of its dam.

So far the deer that follow their paths through our woods and across our driveway have not bothered our gardens at all. I don't think they considered our vegetable or flower gardens worth it last summer. They do nibble the tips of the branches of our apple trees in winter. I watched a buck, a doe, and two fawns walking cautiously in single file across our field one summer morning. It was a lovely sight. We have several secret spots in our woods just like the one I described in this book. They are complete with lichen, moss, pine needles, and piles of deer droppings.

We like to hunt for animal tracks in the snow. It amazes us how much activity goes on behind our backs in the woods at night or during twilight. When we first spotted a snowshoe hare it was in its in-between stage of coloration. Since then we have seen it all brown and all white.

On page ninety-three of *The Family Butterfly Book* there is a beautiful, more than life-size photograph of a mourning cloak. I read about the mourning cloak before I saw my first one, so when I eventually did spot one I was excited. It was the first butterfly to show itself in spring and the last to accompany me in autumn. One fluttered around me as I dug holes for my daffodil bulbs. Bumblebees and American coppers cover the thyme in our herb garden in summer.

Around the middle of the summer we had a dark cloud drop sleet

Afterword

on us. The chickens were dismayed and took cover. Later there was the brightest and most complete rainbow we had ever seen. That week I added the sleet and the rainbow to my story.

The weather is fickle in Maine and the summer nights so cool that tomatoes only do well in lots of manure and with a definite head start indoors in spring. We went swimming in a lake a few days before Labor Day when the temperature was a nice hot eighty-five degrees. Two days later we awoke to frost on the ground and ice in a dish left on the lawn. All of our ripening tomatoes were ruined. All but the carrots and some herbs were lost to us because we didn't cover anything. The carrots only grew an inch long after months of being in the ground. My son finally harvested them in October and suggested we serve them as hors d'oeuvres. From now on, since I am a transplant to Maine, I will try to predict the threat of a late summer frost through the soles of my feet the night before — like Emma — or pay more attention to the weather broadcast.

I'm sure that there are lots of towns called Appleton across the Northern states, perhaps thanks to Johnny Appleseed — the name given to John Chapman (1774-1847). We have thirteen old apple trees on our property and hope to revive some of them. The prettiest tree overlooks the cemetery. Near it thrives a large patch of lily-of-the-valley that probably were tossed into our woods by a visitor many years back. A memorial service was held in the cemetery last May. Pastor spoke and prayed. We all sang "America the Beautiful," a quartet sang, and our girls played songs on their string instruments. We've had house guests from the South comment on how our rural town seems to be somewhat stuck in the past.

Our woods surround three sides of the cemetery and are strewn with years of accumulated glass and plastic containers that once held flowers. Much of the glass is shattered into sharp pieces and the plastic flowers haven't disintegrated. We guess that if we collected all the glass and plastic from our woods it would fill a dozen extra-large trash bags. This is not an exaggeration and it is the reason we haven't yet attempted this chore. Last Christmas my son asked me if I liked how he had decorated a present. I said I did. Then he told me that he had found his plastic poinsettia at the cemetery. I managed to control my inclination to recoil at the thought of my son as a grave robber. Then he told me he

Afterword

found it in the woods and that meant his piece of plastic was a frugal bit of recycling. I felt better.

There is much more nature in New England (and wherever you live) than was described in this story. Not all of the nature we observed even last year could fit into this book. An elegant luna moth was found resting by our back porch light. A humming bird was spotted in the garden. I came across a ruffed grouse under some trees. I kept my eyes on it for half a minute before it scurried to a different hiding place. My eldest daughter discovered moose footprints all along the edge of our wet dirt driveway in autumn. We were all impressed to see the tracks, but hope we don't bump into one as we are whizzing up our snowy driveway some foggy winter's night. I awoke one autumn morning to a chipmunk's squeaky chatter and a blue jay's shrill cry. One look out my bedroom window showed me what they were complaining about. A flock of black wild turkeys was feeding on our lawn. If the chickens had been out of their coop, Fanny, the hen at the top of the pecking order, would have chased the bunch of them into the woods. I say this because she did just that on a summer's eve when the same flock ventured onto the yard. The other frightened chickens hid under our car.

No matter what the habitat and weather in your area, your Nature Notebook can be filled with unique finds.

I spend time outdoors whenever I can. A dozen insect bites any given day in summer will prove it. I understand the term Natural Revelation and believe that nature is one way God reveals himself to us. Creation is a doctrine of the church and is reflected in the hymns I chose for this book.

~

Walking Trails and Botanical Gardens

~

Most of the places we have lived have provided us with a small backyard. A Sunday drive would bring us to a park where we could walk

Afterword

in some woods. I remember one such walking trail near Nashville, Tennessee, on which we met a man who was looking for a Rufus-sided towhee (a Mr. Murphy character). He let us look through his binoculars at one. They only come out in the open in mating season, he told us. There was a lady walking in front of us on the trail who was wearing strong perfume. I would have preferred smelling something more akin to a walk through the woods. Well, that's what I was thinking at the time until we came upon a stagnant pond with a row of turtles basking on a log. What odorous beasts! At that moment I would have preferred the perfume of the strange lady.

We used to take walks in Fair Hill, Maryland, through a covered bridge and wade in the stream it crossed. Taking a bag of crisp juicy apples with us became our simple picnic tradition. My younger daughter would eye with envy those who took the trail on horseback.

In Oregon we would often head out to Mt. Pisgah. There, in the middle of the walking path, we witnessed a snake in the process of swallowing a mole. It was also the only place we ever saw the wild fawn lily.

When we visited my parents in Florida we went on a nature trail and watched armadillos lumber across our path without any fear of us. The vegetation was very different from what we were used to seeing.

Botanical gardens are a treat to visit. There may be one in your area. Most of the plants are labeled, which is a boon to those who remember to bring their Nature Notebooks. Less common plants can be found at a botanical park. There may even be varieties of plants not found in your field guide. And in the winter a greenhouse is a welcome place.

⌇

What? No Car, No Television, No Computer?

⌇

Perhaps one reason I chose the 1930s for the time of my story was to be able to write scenes that were conveniently free of television or computer games. This thought only occurred to me after the story was already in progress. It also occurred to me much later that Carol doesn't

Afterword

have her own car, nor does she drive. This was typical for many women of the time, but it was also the case in my life. As I have mentioned before in other writings, my husband took our one family car to work and I was — sort of — marooned at home with my little children from Monday through Friday. Rarely was an afternoon spent in traffic rushing to outside appointments (unless one of us had a dental appointment and I drove my husband to work, or took a taxi). All shopping was done on Saturdays or evenings. Sunday afternoon was usually not spent shopping or sitting in a crowded restaurant, but on naturewalks with Dad or sharing a home-cooked meal with friends. Music lessons outside the home were started much later — when my first child was twelve years old and when a second car was available to us. Consequently life was simple — and a lot less hectic. Homeschooling was a natural development for us, because we were used to being home together. If your cry is that "we have no time for such things as nature study," one reason could be that you are too busy outside the home.

~

The Erosion of Neighborhood Play

~

The six points listed in the Supplement (and which are explained more fully in *Home Education*) are intended to precede what Miss Mason believed children should learn, and how they should be taught. One reason I included them in the Supplement was to emphasize their importance and to show by shining contrast how much time so many children spend indoors — immovable — behind a school desk, in front of the television, computer, or in the car. My mother regularly chased her children outdoors. I think we were outdoors more than we were indoors when school was let out for the year. (This was one way she kept her house clean and tidy, I think.) In winter we enjoyed less time outdoors, and yet when it snowed we took full advantage of it. I remember, however, that we were fastidiously bundled up to the point that the range

Afterword

of motion in our limbs was significantly restricted. Even making a snow-angel took effort.

A friend once wrote me that the other mothers in her neighborhood could guess what book she had been reading aloud to her children by what could be heard next-door: the playing out of the story in tree, in wagon, in makeshift costume, with props or without. My children have been known to do the same. Looking back, I grew up with hopscotch, jump-rope, dolls pushed in carriages, making forts in the woods in summer and snow-forts in winter, bicycling back and forth on the block, jumping through the backyard sprinkler, roller skating, ice skating, sledding, all with neighborhood children. We ran from backyard to backyard. There were no fences to separate us — only a few shrubs and trees. We sang and swung on each others' squeaky swing sets.

From age six to age seventeen none of the neighborhood children I played with moved away. None of us had mothers who worked full time out of the home. (Almost all of them were frugal stay-at-home mothers.) Eating out at the local New Jersey diner was a rare treat. (We ate out once a year.) Not one of the married couples had gotten a divorce. Not one of the fathers made a career change. There were white collar and blue collar workers. None of the children ever used a swear word. Until the high school years we had never heard of swear words. (Can you believe it?) All of the families except one attended a place of worship once a week. There was a range of faiths represented. I am amazed when I think back on those days (the 60s and 70s). I enjoyed the kind of neighborhood activity described and preserved for us in Eleanor Estes' "Moffat" books. I was blessed with much, but I didn't know how much, at the time.

How different it has been for my children in the neighborhoods where we have lived. (We can count on both hands the number of neighborhoods we have lived in, mostly renting.) I wanted this same storybook neighborhood experience for my children, but my dreams and hopes for it were never realized. Why did the neighborhoods our family lived in seem so lifeless, the children so unimaginative and rude — or worse, profane? I don't know what we would have done without the homeschooling community to connect with. Sorrowful thoughts come to mind when I think about how easily bored, and preoccupied with promiscuity, so many of America's children are today. The breakdown of the fam-

Afterword

ily, the amoral public schools, the subtle deliberate slant of the newscasts on the major networks, Christianity and vice made the subject of laughter on television, the liberal agenda of Hollywood, all contribute greatly to the decline of our civilization.

I believe Christian parents are contributing something different, something eternally better. Today in our country it is no small task to raise up godly offspring for His pleasure and to be good citizens. It is a task that starts with dedication. All the many little things you do for your family are not trite. They will count as a very big thing in the long run. Your giving, your leading, and your teaching are the hope for America. Christian parents dedicated to family are the hidden heroes of today's society. And in the midst of our exertion, let us not grow weary or be anxious. Rather, let us consider the lilies and how they grow.

Karen. July 2001

The photo shows Emma Cook, my great-great-grandmother, holding my mother, Joan, in her arms. It was taken on July 11, 1934, on the occasion of my mother's first birthday.

Endnotes

CHAPTER 3: GIVING THE GOLDENROD ANOTHER TRY

1. Charlotte Mason, *Home Education* (Union, Maine: Charlotte Mason Research & Supply, 2001), 64. *Home Education* was first published in 1886.

CHAPTER 6: A CONGREGATION OF SWALLOWS

1. Anna Botsford Comstock, *Handbook of Nature Study* (Ithaca, N.Y.: Cornell University Press, 1967), 15.

CHAPTER 9: CONTRAPTIONS

1. Comstock, *Handbook*, 232.

Endnotes

CHAPTER 10: PUMPKINS

1. John Greenleaf Whittier, "The Pumpkin."

CHAPTER 11: IT'S ASLEEP, ISN'T IT?

1. Comstock, *Handbook*, 390.

CHAPTER 28: MARVELOUS SNOWFLAKES

1. Alberta V. Shute, *A Year and a Day on the Farm* (North Manchester, Maine: Balm O'Gilead Press, 1972), 16.
2. "Almanac: December," *Country Journal* (Nov/Dec 2000), 14. "A self-educated farmer from Jericho, Vermont, Wilson 'Snowflake' Bently (1865-1931) attracted world attention for his pioneering work in photomicrography. In 1885 he became the first person to photograph a single snowflake." *Snow Crystals* is a collection of his photographs taken in the 1920s.

CHAPTER 29: MICHAEL'S SPEECH

1. Mary Wilder Tileston, *Daily Strength for Daily Needs* (New York: G. P. Putnam's Sons, 1928), 170.

CHAPTER 34: WHEN DAFFODILS BEGIN TO PEER

1. Shakespeare, *The Winter's Tale*, 4,3.

CHAPTER 38: KNOWLEDGE FOR KNOWLEDGE'S SAKE

1. Mason, *Home Education*, 144.

CHAPTER 40: TULIPS

1. Colonial Dames of America, *Herbs and Herb Lore of Colonial America* (New York: Dover Publications, 1995), 29. Even though

this book was not published in Carol's day, the information could have been available to her.

CHAPTER 42: THE DARLING BUDS OF MAY

1. From Shakespeare's Sonnet 18: "Shall I compare thee to a summer's day?"

CHAPTER 47: GOODBYE TO BRIDGETON

1. Shakespeare, *Richard II*, 2, 1.

CHAPTER 48: EMMA COOK'S GARDEN

1. Constance Rourke, *Audubon* (New York: Harcourt Brace and Company, 1936), 11-12.

CHAPTER 49: BIBLIOMANIA

1. Robert Herrick, "To the Virgins," in *The Standard Book of English and American Verse*, selected by Nella Braddy (Garden City, New York: Garden City Publishing Company, 1932), 109-110.

CHAPTER 52: OUT IN THE FIELDS WITH GOD

1. Jethro Kloss, *Back to Eden* (Santa Barbara, California: Woodbridge Press Publishing Co, 1975), 296.
2. Marianne Haug Gjersvik, *Green Fun — Plants as Play* (New York: Firefly Books, 1981), 31.

CHAPTER 55: FARM HANDS

1. Rick Mikula, *The Family Butterfly Book* (Powhal, Vermont: Storey Books, 2000), 8.

CHAPTER 57: THE RAIN IS RAINING ALL AROUND

Endnotes

1. Robert Louis Stevenson, "Rain," in *A Child's Garden of Verses*.

CHAPTER 58: A SPOON WITH ROSES ON THE HANDLE

1. Mason, *Home Education*, 304.
2. Bobby J. Ward, *A Contemplation Upon Flowers — Garden Plants in Myth and Literature* (Portland, Oregon: Timber Press, 1999), 75. This excerpt is from the poem "Buttercups and Daisies," by Eliza Cook, who was a Victorian poet.
3. "The Fairyland of Science," *My Book House*, vol. 6, edited by Olive Beaupré Miller (Chicago: The Book House for Children, 1937), 184. Although my copy of *My Book House* was published in 1937, the first edition was published in 1920, and it was this edition that Emma had on her library shelves.

Publisher's Resources

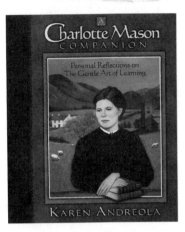

A Charlotte Mason Companion
Personal Reflections on
the Gentle Art of Learning
By Karen Andreola, 374 pages,
beautifully illustrated
$18.95 ❧ 1-889209-02-3

~

Simply Grammar
An Illustrated Primer
By Karen Andreola, 178 pages,
Victorian illustrations
$24.95 ❧ 1-889209-01-5

~

The Original Homeschooling Series
By Charlotte Mason, 2400 pages, 6-vol. set
$58.95 ❧ 1-889209-00-7